THE REVOLUTION OF SELF-LOVE

A YEARLONG JOURNEY OF SELF-LOVE: 52 AUTHORS, STORIES AND EXCERSISES

THE LITTLE VOLCANO
AUTHORS COLLECTIVE

rosie@thelittlevolcano.com

Published by TheLittleVolcano.com

Contents

COMMITMENT OF SELF-LOVE

Self-love without action is just theory, and self-love in action is transformation.

By: Kit Volcano

Story:

It is 1 a.m. and I'm walking down the cold, blustery Chicago street. I'm wrapped up in a scarf, shivering, crying and slipping around on the frozen sidewalks. I'm in a tunnel vision of despair and pain.

My shop is at the ground level of the tallest building in the neighborhood. Head hung low to avoid the eye contact of people leaving the bars, I take myself up to the rooftop via the elevator.

I'm a complete emotional wreck. In the past 6 months, I've lost what little respect I had for myself, and in my eyes, I'm completely unlovable. I'm sobbing, pacing, and I keep seeing all the mistakes I've made in my life, over and over and over again. I keep seeing how I will never be loved. I didn't see much hope for myself, so I made the decision to end my life.

I'm pacing back and forth on the rooftop. I called every single lifeline on my phone, and no one picked up. I so desperately wanted to jump, but holding me back was a tiny, dim spark of life buried within me. It lit up and whispered in the smallest voice. What it said that night saved my life.

What that voice said put me on the path of finding deep self-love, discovering it reflected back to me in my incredible marriage and now doing my life's work: coaching, hosting events, writing books, and changing lives of people who are ready to step up fully to the plate and live.

It said, "But you haven't even lived yet." I realized at that moment that I had been living so much to win the love of others, that I had never lived for myself. I thought that the love of someone else would be the thing that completed me. All I ever wanted was a soulmate, someone to marry, someone who would be in love with me forever and fill up all the holes of emptiness within me.

My belief system at the time said, "The only way you can love yourself is if it is validated by the love of someone else." This led me into relationships and friendships where I sacrificed my needs, desires, and self-identity for the approval of someone else. I never let myself fully discover who I was because I needed to know I was lovable before I could even face it. This type of thinking brought me to the end of my rope.

It was my wake up call. That was a moment when a great decision had to be made. I was about to end my life, still waiting for the acceptance of someone else, having never truly lived, or loved myself.

I stepped away from that ledge with an ultimatum to myself. Instead of jumping off that building, I would leap into the scary unknown of loving myself. I would finally listen to the calling of my spirit instead of doing what I thought others wanted me to do. But I gave myself a deadline, I would go all in, 100%. If after 30 days nothing had changed, I could renegotiate my life.

For the first time in my life, I really truly gave myself permission to live. I did everything I had ever wanted, including some of those things I felt embarrassed to do. I stopped dating. I went to therapy. I read self-help books, I got psychic readings, I stopped spending money on drinking, I stopped hanging out with people that I felt shitty around. Weeks soon turned into months. I did yoga, I got energy healing, I started meditating. I traveled by myself. I biked in the rain. I danced to the music in my headphones in the grocery store. I grew a garden and I fed myself from it.

I stopped giving a fuck. I listened to every little nudge of my spirit, and I said yes. I fell in love with being me. I filled every single hole inside myself with self-love, and I developed a deep connection to my purpose for being alive.

That same voice that saved my life on that building nine years ago also spoke up and said "Write this book. Self-love is going to change the world." That same voice that spoke up inside me lives inside all of the authors that contributed to this book. Their inner voices spoke up and said, "Tell your story. Love yourself enough to know your story will change the life of at least one person who reads it."

Reader, we as a wild gang of self-love warriors, know that that one person can be you. Now you don't have to be at the end of your rope, suicidal, or depressed for this book to change your life for the better. I never wish depression or that much pain on anyone. It was, however, my gift that I was finally in so much pain, that I had no other choice, but to be me, and to love me.

Everyone's journey to self-love looks different. For some, it may come much later in life: it's a heart attack, the loss of a child, a divorce, or a life-threatening illness. For others, it may be much simpler.

Now I want to sincerely ask you; What are you waiting for to fully love yourself? Are you waiting until everything gets destroyed, so you have no other choice? Are waiting until you reach the brink of losing something before you realize it's preciousness? Are you waiting for the fight with your family or your partner that finally makes you snap? What will *force* you to make a great decision to follow the voice inside that is begging you to focus on what's important?

That breath you just took, feel it. That means you still have something inside. You're still here for a reason. How long can you go on pretending that you're not important enough in this world to be fully loved? Take this as your wake up call. Will you say, "YES" to loving yourself deeper this year?

Some of the most successful people are successful because they had hit such a hard bottom, that they had a serious reason to change. We want to impress upon you, that it doesn't have to take you hitting rock bottom to create an amazing life; it can be a good book, a fantastic community and some accountability to keep you focused.

This book is for anyone and everyone whose lives can be profoundly changed by a year-long journey of Self-Love. A journey that will lead you to a deep, purpose-rich, expansive, connected, beautiful life.

This book is the collective stories of 52 authors who share their journey with self-love. My soulmate, partner in crime and co-author, Rosie Volcano and I birthed this book into existence with a massive flash of impetus and inspiration. From the moment we both decided it would happen, to sending the final draft off to press, only two months had passed. As you open this book and trace your eyes across every word, we pass that same energy on to you. We hold steady to the belief that lightning will strike for you in the same way it has for us. If you want that same flash of aliveness to come into your life, your job is now simple. All you have to do is know that there is something more that you want out of life, and commit to going on a year-long journey of self-love with us.

Every week a different author tells their story of coming to a great moment of self-love. Every week you will be inspired by the intimate stories of people from around the world. We have stories of cancer, career shifts, relationships, loss, vulnerability, healing and each story takes you on a self-love adventure. These authors have thoughtfully and heartfully crafted each chapter to impact you. At the end of each chapter, there is an exercise for you to do that week, because self-love without action is just theory, and self-love in action is transformation.

Intro Exercise: Commit to Self-Love

To join this journey follow these steps:

Step One: Commitment

Write your name and your commitment inside of this book.

I ______________________ commit to a year long journey of loving myself. I commit to read the weekly chapter and complete the weekly exercise.

X ______________________________________

Step Two: Assessment

In the back of the book there are a series of pages that will be your before and after snapshots.

You will come back to these pages periodically as a way to stand back and see how far you've come.

When you finish this journey you will have a compelling synopsis of your year reminding you of the progress you have made.

I encourage you to actually write in this book. Make it messy, write in the margins, make this book a living document of your journey.

If you don't have a physical copy, print out the pdf of the writing exercises from the website, or follow along with a journal.

Turn to page _______to start your beginning snapshot. Then come back here and return to step three.

Step Three: Connect

We have built a community of people united in this work: a digital home of connection, vulnerability, depth, joy, support, and friendship.

Thousands of others from around the world are joining in on this journey together. People from all over the globe, including the authors, are going through this book week by week in a private facebook group.

Share your journey with others.

Experience the power of accountability.

Connect to the authors.

Get everything you need from our websites:

Thelittlevolcano.com
or
Therevolutionofselflove.com

Step Four: Invite a Friend to Join You

Whether you invite your closest friend or your whole facebook list, bring someone along on this self-love ride. You are the sum of the company you keep. Life becomes better and easier when the people around you are growing in the same positive, expansive, beautiful ways that you are. It's never too late to ask a friend to go on this journey together, to take a stand for those that you love, and to change their life too.

Here are some easy ways to invite them:

1. Buy them a copy of the book
2. Text them
3. Call them
4. Start a book club and guilt them into coming

Step Five: Share Your Journey on Social Media

Self-love is often bold, unapologetic and attractive. It naturally leaves a visible trail for others to follow. If you start to feel so alive from this journey that you want to share it with others we have created a hashtag just for that purpose.

#revolutionofselflove

Step Six:

Come back each week for a new piece of the adventure, and if you get off track, just come back.

Winging It

Practice Makes for Better Practice

By: Aydian Dowling

Story:

Within this book, you're going to read many accounts of self-love and self-compassion. There will be stories of heroism where you are taken on a journey to the depths of sadness and come out the other end with wings that drip of gold. There will be stories of less intensity, where stillness and patience are the lessons to learn. Some stories you will relate to, and others not so much. Make sure you lean into the ones that you do connect with. Re-read those ones. Each journey or tale will have your mind embellished with jewels of knowledge and hopefully leave you feeling ready to take action.

This chapter is a bit different. This chapter is filled with the illusions of self-doubt, unworthiness, and the scariest of all, pure realness. That is because I am the part of this book that reminds you that behind every word you read, is a person who is still practicing the craft of self-love. The bubble being burst is, no one has it all figured out. Everyone is purely a practitioner of their self-love craft. We all have to deal with the missteps, the regrets, and the straight up mess-ups.

The biggest illusion of pure self-love is that you aren't allowed to mess up or have a bad day. That if you genuinely had self-love, then all your choices would leave you feeling amazing and empowered. You would never look at yourself with regret or anger again. Fortunately, that is not true. I say fortunately because with more exploration and practice comes new awareness and with new awareness comes new depth and with new depth comes even truer happiness and love of self.

Self-love is the acceptance of all your emotions from the sadness and anger to the joy and fulfillment. The happiness that comes when you love yourself has much more depth than rainbows and glitter. It's a happiness that is well-rounded in disappointment and fear, which make way for a clearer path to satisfaction and peace.

So as everyone in this book shares their journey, we remember that no one is perfect and that practice makes for better practice. I had to learn this part just like everyone else. I thought that I would hit some kind of breaking point where self-love would radiate from my being, and I would never have a bad or self-limiting day again. I knew it wouldn't happen overnight, I just didn't know it would be a continuing practice for the rest of my life. I swore there was a threshold that I could burst past, where I'd be able to leave all this unworthiness behind me once and for all. I just wanted to be the person who had it all figured out. Who was able to move through life unbothered by outside forces, be at full peace with myself, and know what lies ahead of me. I wanted to be like Oprah. She always looks like she has it together; she knows what's up. But I've come to learn, she's just winging it.

I once heard a quote from a movie, I'm paraphrasing here: "Just go out there and wing it, like everybody else." This phrase really got to me. Like a brick to the face out of nowhere, got to me. It made me realize that no matter who is doing what, they are purely winging it. That yes, a brain surgeon can go to college, and get straight A's, make discoveries, and all of that jazz. But the one thing they cannot do is know the outcome of the future. This means that every single incision they make is them purely winging it. They get their gloves on, put on their masks make the first cut and hope that what they have practiced day in and day out will help guide them to the answer they are looking for. Not knowing what's behind the surface, unable to predict, hail-mary style winging it.

Now don't get freaked out about your doctors or surgeons; that's not the point. The point is that those same surgeons are successful more often than not. From the surgeons to the honestly winging it, high flying pilots, most every time, everyone arrives home safely. The truth is there should be no fear in winging it. Winging it is an action that is made up of all your past practices. So yes, you're winging it, but you're also making an active choice based on what the outcomes in your past have led you to.

Which brings me back to the point of this chapter. No one person in this book has it right; we all have it right. Because each one of us wakes up every single day and does our very best to make choices that make us feel good. Based on how that choice made us feel, we make more choices. The choice to not get up early, to skip meditation, or pass on going for a walk, has left us feeling not as satisfied. It has left us feeling ungrounded and leads to the mismanagement of our time and emotions. So we make a choice to get up and actually meditate, or make ourselves a healthy breakfast, or get some fresh morning air and take a walk outside. We learned from our past practices, and we try every single day again to welcome more and more self-love into our lives.

We are winging it because we don't know what the outcome of every single instance is going to be. We are all human, and we encounter things that throw us off track. We don't know what's right beneath the surface before we make our first cut. We have assumptions, we try to prepare, but at the end of the day, we just do not know what is behind every door. We only know what we have practiced in the past that has left us feeling good or bad. Every time we make a choice, we are practicing for the future.

Don't be fooled. We are not guru's, masters, or preachers. We are practitioners sharing the stories of our journey, and why we feel these actions, when made into a practice, may help you in your own continuing journey to self-love.

Weekly Exercise

Practice makes for better practice. This week is about experimenting and practicing.

1. Pick two things you've wanted to start doing. Things you felt when you heard or read about them, you think 'Ohh I need to do this!'
2. Out of the 7 days this week, do one of them the first three days and the following the second set of three days.
3. Each one of those days, take 1-2 minutes and jot down all your rawest emotions from that day. Was it easy to do or hard to get into? Did you feel better, worse or the same after completing it? Get honest and don't stop writing until your 2 minutes are up. Just write and write. There is no judgment on what you write, your spelling or your grammar.
4. On that 7th day, sit and spend a few minutes comparing the two activities you have done over the past 6 days. Which do you think you enjoyed more, based on your entries? Which was the most easeful in your mind? Which did you want to do that 7th day if you couldn't do both?
5. Now take that choice, and do it for another week. Don't give up until you hit that next 7th day. Do you still like it?

The first point of this exercise is to learn how to practice something over and over without expecting some huge accomplishment besides just the practice of practice.

The second point is to acknowledge what practices make you feel good and which make you feel bad. Once you know, you stop doing what you feel bad doing and you do more of what makes you feel good.

Even if you don't feel like an expert in meditation, create an altar or a vision board. Take 10 minutes and look up a video of how-to. Don't get too caught up in the details, and go after it. You don't need a meditation pillow, the perfect meditation music, or the perfect lit candle to start meditating. Just get into the intention and wing it.

The Power of Introspection

How Exploring My Inner World Gave Me a New Life

By: Mayra Garcia

Story:

"If this is going to be my life, I'd rather not live." This thought lived with me every single day for years. I'd think to myself, "This can't be it." I felt hopeless and lost. Every day was a struggle and something to "get through." I did my best to stay afloat and not descend into that debilitating, dark, and deep abyss of despair and depression. These thoughts consumed me, and I feared to live my life this way.

In an attempt to "fix" myself I began doing all the things I thought I was supposed to do to be a happy, functioning member of society because clearly, something was wrong with me. Or so I thought. So, I read self-help books, listened to motivational videos, rejected negative thoughts, and only allowed myself to speak positive things. But behind that positive band-aid was a bleeding wound, one that no matter how much I tried to bullshit myself, would not heal or disappear. I was pretending to be something I was not; happy.

On the surface, I was one of the most positive people I knew. Those close to me considered me a happy individual; always smiling and optimistic. They didn't know that deep inside I was crying, begging to be seen. They weren't aware of the hidden wounds and inner battles I was bearing and fighting internally. I didn't want them to know because I believed I'd be seen as a depressing person, I'd become a burden, and I'd be rejected. So, I kept to myself. The mask of that positive persona kept me chained to a life that I felt wasn't worth living. I believed there were so many things wrong with me and I became obsessed with trying to "fix" myself. The problem was that I was lost, I didn't know why I felt the way I did, or how to change it.

The feelings of despair weighed down on me like a ton of bricks, and the thoughts of suicide crossed my mind so many times that I was in constant fear that I'd eventually succumb. I wasn't good enough to be loved and was in a continual need to prove myself worthy. I was sinking into a place that I knew I didn't belong. I deserved better and wanted desperately to pull myself out. I felt so low, but thankfully I chose to listen to that voice that told me things could get better. I was forced to do some deep self-reflection, and take an honest look at myself—something I had avoided for such a long time.

I was afraid of what those feelings would reveal about me. I didn't want to be imperfect; I didn't want to accept that I didn't have it "all together," or that I was flawed in some way. I didn't want to see those defects and admit to them because it would place me in a position of vulnerability. And being vulnerable meant losing my grip and control of how I'd be perceived, how well I'd be accepted, and how much I'd be loved. I feared rejection so much that I people-pleased my way into relationships. I would offer to give a friend a ride even if it meant being late to class. I would agree to babysit even if it meant I'd have to leave work early. I would lend that relative money even if it meant I would be broke for the next week, or I would stay quiet when someone was rude or hurtful towards me for the sake of keeping the peace.

I was so desperate to be liked and accepted by others that I avoided healthy boundaries like the plague. They weren't "my thing." Boundaries were like that one ex. You know, the kind of ex you have one of those nasty/hate-your-guts/never-want-to-see-you breakups with? I believed boundaries were like love repellent. How is saying, "No," not agreeing to everything, or not putting everyone else's needs before mine going to help me gain their love and approval?

Then, it hit me. I was miserable in my own existence because I didn't love myself. I didn't know how to, and because of this, I searched for external validation. I kept putting others before myself because I thought I needed to do, give, or be something other than who I was to be accepted. How in the world was I ever going to be comfortable with myself if I wasn't being true to myself? How could I make myself happy if I didn't know what I really wanted? I was always more concerned about everyone else and their needs because I needed their love; because I was missing my own. I had abandoned myself and was choosing instead to be who everyone else wanted or needed me to be. It was that moment that I realized I needed my own love, respect, and approval.

That realization led me to one of the most important questions I've ever asked myself, and one that has changed my life for the better. I began questioning what I wanted and needed in those moments that I sought the love and approval of others, and began finding those things within myself. I stopped putting myself last and started questioning my intentions with those around me. I made it a habit to stop and ask what was in my best interest anytime I felt my people-pleasing ways creeping up, and I began honoring that. I stopped accepting people's poor behavior towards me and began removing myself from those people, places, or things that didn't serve me. I eliminated "friendships" that were one-sided and toxic in my life, and I learned to say, "No" when necessary.

The truth is, we don't need to be someone different than who we already are to be loved and accepted. We don't need to do or give anything that we don't feel in our hearts for others to appreciate us. You are already enough, you are already loved, and you are already worthy just by being you. Exploring my inner wants and needs gave me a special intimacy with myself that I so eagerly yearned for, and it gave me the freedom to be true to who I really am. We will always be a work in progress, as perfection is not a human quality. However, we can always choose to walk in the direction of light and love. We can always strive to be a better version of ourselves.

You deserve your own love & acceptance, and you deserve peace, but only you can give yourself that gift. Accepting this truth and the responsibility that comes with it taught me that to grow in my own self-love, I needed to listen to and meet my own needs. I've made it a habit of asking myself these questions every day as they allow me to stay connected to my inner being. I share this exercise with you in the hopes that it will help you explore your inner world—and shed light on the things that are calling for your love and attention—so that you too can escape the need for that empty, external love and validation.

Weekly Exercise

Take time to check in this week. Ask yourself these questions throughout the week:

- What am I feeling right now?
    - Sit in silence and ponder on the emotions and sensations you're experiencing.
- Why do I feel this way?
    - Be completely open and honest with where those emotions are coming from. Reflect on why it's an issue and why it bothers you.
- What do I need?
    - Take full responsibility for your feelings and ask what you can do for yourself to feel better. Remember, your feelings and emotions are no one's responsibility but your own.

- What action can I take to love and care for myself?
    - Determine what you need and set some time in your day to set that action in motion. This is by far the greatest act of self-love.

An Education in the Art of Living

Looking within and doing the inner work has taught me what many books could not: how to love myself (and what is).

By: Callum Doherty

Story:

Reading *The Slight Edge* at the age of eighteen marked the beginning of my self-love journey—although I didn't know this at the time. The book had an immediate impact on me. I became obsessed with the idea of studying great books and thinkers in search of understanding all there is to know about the art of living. I wanted financial freedom, perfect health, and spiritual enlightenment. I thought that the key to success across these domains could be found through a commitment to learning. After reading that book, I ordered twenty books on personal development. And so, began my very own Hero's quest.

Over the next few years, my habits began to change, and I became more health conscious and accrued knowledge in personal development. After years of searching for answers and working on my health, I still felt as though I was missing something. For all my hard work, I didn't feel any happier. In fact, life had become less fun, I laughed less, and was more disconnected in my relationships than when I started the self-improvement journey. I now see the issue was the underlying narrative and stories I was telling myself—albeit at an unconscious level. The story was centered around a general belief that I was a person of great potential but has always underachieved.

I have always had a sense of my infinite potential. Growing up this sense bordered on the overconfident and arrogant. Then somewhere along the way, I lost this self-assurance. This self-aggrandizing attitude now served me as a cover-up to a more negative self-image. This underlying narrative is a tough one to live with as it creates such high standards that are impossible to maintain. All my shortcomings and failures served to strengthen the voice of this inner critic.

I had studied, exercised and even investigated starting a business, but inside I felt empty. I was looking for the answers in the external world, but I now see that I was really searching to *feel* better. I even identified 'spiritual enlightenment' as one of my initial goals, although I wasn't sure intellectually why I wanted this or even what it was.

Now I see that nobody, not even the Buddha or the Christ, achieves enlightenment and lives happily ever after. What both ancient wisdom and neuroscience suggest is that enlightenment is a state of being, it's emotional and in the domain of feeling. And like all states of being, it is transient and oscillates; it can only be experienced at the moment. What we are really after is to live a string of enlightened moments.

How liberating! I realized that I was looking outside of myself in pursuit of an internal goal: to live in higher emotional states more frequently. I do not see my time as wasted, for all my questing led me to the level of self-awareness which brought this very realization. It doesn't mean at all that my work is done. In fact, now the real inner work can begin. I used to believe that it was my ignorance and lack of knowledge which held me back from living to my full potential. Now I see the intellect and knowledge for what it is: an excellent tool. Like our technological advancements, our rational minds are great, but we cannot allow them to run our lives unchecked.

Recently, my tutor asked my class a thought-provoking question. True to form, I tried to come up with an answer. He smiled and said to me, "It's okay to say, 'I don't know'!" This light-hearted remark struck a chord with me. I began to reflect on how good it feels to say, "I don't know." God, it feels good, to relinquish this innate tendency of the brain to want to know, understand and explain away everything. Ancient wisdom will tell you that 'don't know mind' is where it's at. In this childlike way of being, you make space for emotional states of wonder, awe, fascination, and amazement. Life becomes more beautiful, and one experiences first-hand the underlying magic of reality. When I let go of this need to know—which is a process—then I make space for feeling. Feeling is fundamental as it brings us fully into the present moment, which is all we have anyway.

At its essence, we are all playing the game of brain and body chemistry. Our minds are spectacular machines. We have more control over our biochemistry than we think. Yet we spend our time playing the wrong games for the wrong reasons. Much of our time is spent with a focus on the external world which only ever produces a small impact on our internal biochemistry. The quest for money, achievement, fame, recognition, etc. may create these higher states of emotion in some people, some of the time. However, it seems an ineffective and altogether strange way of playing the game of life.

So how does one go about creating this desirable brain chemistry which leads to more moments of enlightenment? The good news is that we all have a great influence on our biochemistry. Act as if you already have it and live in a way that increases the likelihood that you will feel good. If you show warmth, tenderness, and compassion to yourself, both in sentiment and in action, then your body will respond. This is the magic; you have everything available to you already and more.

My message is this: We are all hugely capable and powerful beings. Naturally, we are endowed with unknown and limitless potential. So, treat yourself as such. Be kind to yourself, give yourself space and room to grow. Our goals are all insignificant if we cannot access and live in the state of love. James Allen said, "Dreams are the seedlings of realities" and like all seeds, your dreams must be cared for and nurtured if they are to flourish.

When you look after and care for yourself deeply, you begin to hold your best interests at heart. I cannot think of any higher form of self-love than this.

"Love doesn't just sit there, like a stone, it has to be made, like bread; remade all the time, made new."
— Ursula K. Le Guin, The Lathe of Heaven

Weekly Exercise

Here are three micro-practices to make self-love a daily practice. These practices are deceptively simple but hugely influential.

Practice radical forgiveness

1. To begin, spend 1-2 minutes thinking about and feeling any anger you feel towards yourself (or another) for any actions of the past that have had a negative impact upon you, however trivial this act may seem.
2. Visualize this younger version of yourself (or another) standing in front of you and exercise empathy and loving sentiments towards them. Seek to understand at a deep compassionate level what it is that made them do it.
3. Finally, envision yourself hugging this person. Repeat and practice this process often.

Realize that you are enough and remind yourself often

- Write it everywhere and say it often to yourself (and others). Open up to the possibility of living a life unhindered by doubt, criticism, and judgment.

Practice being present

- Create internal space and serenity through this practice. Leave your eyes open, bring awareness on the breath and inhale deeply, open up the jaw and release any tension that you may be holding in the jaw/face. Now rest your gaze upon any object in front of you and study the purpose. Hold your attention on the object for a minimum of 6 deep breaths.

From a Teenager to a Woman

How I Took the Driver's Seat Back from My 14-Year-Old Self

By: Este Webster

Story:

"Fatty."

I still remember his voice, his face filled with freckles, his sandy blonde hair, and clear gray-blue eyes. He was in my 6th-grade class and sat in front of me. The boy would turn around intermittently and utter this word to me repetitively. I'd sit staring at him, frozen and unable to use my vocal cords. It was like a shock through my system when someone would call me a name, and it happened a lot. I never really knew what to say. I heard all kinds of variations of weight-related taunts growing up: fatty, fatass, whale, pig, ogre, Shrek, gorda, underwear girl (that was fun), slut, weirdo, freak, loser.

Bullying was something I dealt with most of my life, it was normal and expected. I grew up being raised by my mom, grandma, and aunt. They were my "safe place," the only place I really felt I could be authentic. I experienced a lot of affirmation when I was home, and then at school, I would hear that I was weird, unlikable, and unacceptable. This hurt, but in truth, it confused me more than anything!

Internally, I began taking on these labels as part of who I was. Growing up, I always suspected that I was capable, beautiful, smart, creative, and I didn't seem to understand why so many people didn't see it. I was a very self-aware child, always curious about myself and others.

After a long-winded battle with drama, I ended up leaving public school in resignation before high school. I really didn't want to continue trying to fit in and deal with the perplexing drama (anchoring a large internal resolution). It just wasn't worth it, why give people a chance anymore when it proved to be futile? As 14-year-old me began to stew, little did I know "she" would be running the show for some time. I resolved that I was more content with figuring out how to live life solo, independent of deep connections and intimacy. It worked well for a while until it didn't anymore.

I never wanted others to feel sorry for me because of my experiences; they set quite a foundation for the healing I would come to find. I strategically learned to build walls that would ensure I was safe from more rejection. It was a comfortable illusion and a typical reaction, not a willful response. I learned that when you make yourself a passenger through life, you lose a lot of connection to choice. Remember how I said 14-year-old Este ran the show for much of my life? She was the wounded child inside me who could only view life through the lens of her young experience.

At a point in my life as an adult, I remembered from a young age, that loving myself and others were when I felt most free. I was frustrated, alone, and running out of options. At this point, I had done some work and gained more awareness of my patterns, yet I still felt resistant to the thought of opening up. I was attached to the ideas of fairness and justice and felt that I was losing power by giving something that wasn't "deserved." After all, my lifelong story of being misunderstood and unwanted was familiar, comfortable, and just "me." Why would I let go without kicking and screaming? Well, I kicked and screamed, but I trusted the process.

After realizing the reality I was invested in just didn't work, I eventually started letting up. I explored various healing modalities over a few years. When it came to truly understanding self-love, I learned several key things; the value in being connected with others for support, that vulnerability was how

I obtained *my* freedom, and that self-compassion was the most treasured tool in my journey towards self-love. Compassion was being kind to myself during each step of my journey, especially through the "darkness." The darkness, while at first daunting, became more and more acceptable, and ultimately became a friend.

Opening my heart to love was hard for me. True love is unconditional in essence, a choice, an opening. I discovered that this was actually the path to empowerment and taking control of my life for the first time, versus something that would make me small and invalidated as I feared. To choose to love myself involved taking personal responsibility, which came in many different forms: learning to trust myself so that I could trust others, being honest about where I was living inauthentically, looking at where I laid blame in order to avoid myself, looking at all the areas where I had unresolved pain that could only be resolved by me. All the wounded spots needed to be allowed to breathe, feel, and be expressed!

Spend time in your darkness, it's wanting your love and approval. Don't be afraid of it. When I learned to give space to the process, the shifts had room. There's a quote, "Your trauma may not be your fault, but healing is your responsibility." You must choose to love yourself enough to heal!

One of the most valuable shifts I have learned in this journey is that I alone am responsible for loving and caring for myself and that I have all the power to do so. I began exploring agency in all areas of my life and watched them transform. My self-love isn't dependent on the words, thoughts, actions, or motivations of others, but from what's gained in those quiet spaces with myself. What alchemizes there is something that can't be bought but grows through surrender and willingness. The full approval for myself teaches me that there's nothing wrong or broken about me and that every part is undeniably human, worthwhile, and lovable.

Weekly Exercise

I love writing practices as a way to integrate self-love, especially in the mornings. It helps me process deeply and ground into my day. One of my favorites is making a list of all of the qualities I like, am grateful for, notice, or appreciate about myself. I also find this pretty magical if I'm not feeling particularly inspired towards myself that day.

Here are some examples of what qualities I would place on my list:

- I love my new hairstyle
- I appreciate how thoughtful I am
- I held a boundary today with someone that I don't usually hold
- I give fantastic gifts to people
- I value my alone time
- I really tried my best at work today
- I am a pretty patient person
- I share vulnerably and help others feel permission to
- I help others feel acknowledged
- I bring fun into a room

The reflections can be as simple, profound, specific, random, or as neutral as you want. Whatever comes up for you and leads you towards expressing is okay! Afterward, you will find yourself in a juicy self-awareness shift and more grounded in love.

Light Comes from Darkness

How to Become Your Own Best Friend

By: Swirl Moore

Story:

When I was much younger, I had no idea how to love myself. Mainly because I didn't know myself. I felt like I didn't fit in or belong anywhere, no matter where I was or who I was with, even my family. I had no self-respect nor self-love which lead to me the exploration of a dark path: escapism. By the time I was 15 years old, I had become so clouded and confused about myself—and life in general—that the only way that I could see any type of relief from the pain that I found myself wallowing in was death.

I attempted suicide, and when I woke up I was so angry! I was angry that I didn't get that sweet relief that I thought that death would bring. A doctor came in and told me, "You are very lucky to be alive! In fact, you should be dead, so you must be alive for a reason." This only confused me even more. Lucky to be alive? Be alive for a reason? This didn't make any sense!

Unfortunately, a couple months later I attempted again. This time, I was sure it was going to work but it didn't. When I woke up, again in the hospital, a different doctor said almost the exact same thing: "You must be a very special lady, anybody else who did what you did would be dead. You must have a great purpose in life." Still angry and still confused, I started to wonder, are they right? Am I alive for a reason? I started to evaluate what the doctor said about being special, about having a purpose. I never really thought about having a purpose before. After that experience, I thought, "What am I supposed to do and who am I supposed to be?"

Then it hit me like like a lightning bolt; I realized that it's not about what I'm *supposed* to do or who I am *supposed* to be. No! It is much simpler than that. I had been focused on self-judgment based on others opinions and projections. I was looking outside of myself for the answers. I realized the answers are *within*. I asked myself the real question of self-exploration, "Who am I?". This simple question led me to open and dive deeper in myself. Ultimately finding my light. The light within me. This was a light to guide me on a new path: a path of spirituality and new types of exploration. This was my first awakening.

As I continued asking myself, "Who am I?" one of the answers I heard in my head one day was, "your own best friend." At that moment, I knew that the most important thing that I could do was to befriend myself. I made a commitment to befriend my inner experience, just like I would with any other person. I started to pay attention to myself. I began to ask myself questions. I began to note and remember what it was that I liked, what I preferred, the way I prefered things, what brought me joy, what helped me feel grounded and centered in my being, what helped me to feel nourished physically, mentally, emotionally, and spiritually. I slowly began to define who I am.

By the time I was 23 years old I had succeeded in becoming my own best friend. I knew myself better than I knew anyone else, and better than anyone else knew me. I felt so close to myself I decided that I would marry myself and I had a self-marriage ceremony. I pampered myself; oiling my body, doing my hair and makeup, dressed in a beautiful gown, and even got myself a ring! I looked in the mirror and made vows—vows to always be true to who I am. To never give up on this sacred journey of life and loving myself. I vowed to keep exploring, learning, deepening into trust, showing up and holding myself in the way that only I knew how: with honor and respect. I would always be my number one, put myself first and tend to my own needs and desires. I was the *one*, and for the first time in my life, I belonged to myself fully.

What else was I to do afterward but to have a honeymoon! I went on a Vision Quest. On this quest, I received my name from the Universe, SWIRL. SWIRL is an acronym for Spirituality, Wisdom, Intuition, Reverence, and Love. This is who I am, what I believe in, what I have to share with the world. The day I downloaded my name, I made my third commitment to myself; to embody SWIRL truly and to live a S.W.I.R.L. L.I.F.E — L.I.F.E. being an acronym for, "Living In Full Expression."

Since then, I follow my heart, the synchronicities in life, and the light of my path. I now come from a place of true love for myself when making decisions, taking actions, reflecting on thoughts, and using my words. This way of being has led me to love myself unconditionally and be able to share unconditional love with others. I found the more I love and connect with myself, the more capacity I have for love and connection with others. The suffering of separation fades as I deepen into Oneness. I find it amazing how not only in me but also in the universe, light is created from the darkness.

Weekly Exercise

When you befriend your inner experience, you learn to ground, nourish, and uplift yourself. Learn the things that you like and need so you are able to build self-trust though showing up and holding yourself as only you know how. It is truly only you who knows what you need and how you need it.

1. Make a list of three things that you do to ground and center yourself.
2. Make a list of three things you do to nourish yourself.
3. Make a list of three things you do to uplift yourself.

Refer back to this list whenever you feel ungrounded, unnourished and down about yourself or life.

BONUS EXERCISE: Think about the way you talk to yourself. Would you talk to a friend that way? Begin to actually treat yourself like you would your best friend...because you are!

Fuck Your Resistance

How to Fall in Love with Self-Love

By: Lisa Warwick

Story:

If you are reading this reluctantly, welcome. I see you. I give you a sarcastic namaste and a tip of the hat. The small, scared, child inside of me is reaching out to yours, across space and time and whatever else we imagine holds us apart.

What are you telling yourself when you're resisting this self-love stuff? Here's what I said, when I was really honest about it: "I wanna be fucking done with this. I'm done crying and would much rather go back to where I was a few weeks ago when I thought I was fine. All of this is traumatizing bullshit." All this was cry-yelled at a life coach a few weeks ago. I can be a little dramatic.

After months of weekly life coaching, group sessions, and a transformational life event—which I lied to everyone about and called a yoga retreat—I was ready to stop digging. My life had gotten better, and I was ready to just relax and coast for a while. And then my life coach asked me if I believed I could be loved as much as I love others. And I fucking snapped.

I caught my breath and was asked to close my eyes and listen. When I am really mad, I often see a small feral girl who lives in the woods. She was raised by wolves, scrappy and alone, and is a version of me under very different circumstances. This time, the little child holding a buck knife got close and told me: "You're right to have a temper tantrum. All of this is bullshit because you know it's not true. You know you're loved, and you're scared to admit it. I'm so tired of seeing you exhausted because you're pretending to be weak, or scared, or barely enough, all just to avoid being proud of who you are. Just be fucking proud already. You are going to keep dealing with this, mostly because you are resisting dealing with this." I knew I needed to change.

My temper tantrum reminded me of the ones I used to see my cousins have before bedtime. I would stare at them, bawling, exhausted, raging, while I thought: "Are you fucking kidding me? I have to pop two melatonin to fall asleep at night. You are tired. Your bed is nearby. It's perfect. Did you not see this coming? Bedtime, the thing that happens every night? Why fight against this?"

What would happen if they accepted, fully and completely at that moment, that they will have to sleep eventually? What would happen if they could see that every moment before surrendering to sleep is going to be a little bit of a shit show? Would they still rage against it? Or would they embrace it, walk upstairs, request their favorite bedtime story and blanket, and welcome sleep?

There is nothing wrong with tiny bodies needing rest; there is nothing wrong with working on loving yourself more. There will never be a place where I can stop working on self-love without it having a negative effect on my life. The only thing that will change over time is that I will get better at seeing what I need and loving whatever comes up. Since I have stopped treating self-love like something I might be able to avoid, or having tantrums when it comes up, I can choose how I love myself. It has become as delightful as being tucked in at night and hearing your favorite bedtime story.

Self-love is different from self-care. It is the difference between being *ok* with yourself or truly *celebrating* yourself; between taking a bath to get clean or adding massage oil and flower petals; between biking to work to get exercise or blasting French pop out of a speaker while you ride, yelling "Bonjour" at strangers. It is an art. It is beautiful. It is proactive.

It is telling new stories about myself and my life instead of repeating and dissecting victim stories from my past, claiming I'm processing when I'm really just finding a creative way to shit on myself. I would recommend skipping this kind of self-care and going straight to loving yourself. I am ending my decades-long pattern of taking care of myself just enough to get to *ok*, then slipping back into old habits, and shamefully returning to self-care.

I still feel some resistance. I'm ashamed I have to work on self-love at all. I admire people who never feel the pull to read these books, who are effortlessly happy, who are never driven to Self-Help-Land because of a deep depression or shitty, self-sabotaging patterns. I can hold on to this story about these imaginary, perfect people, and the shame that goes along with it, or I can change my story. The new story I tell is: I grew up in a culture that taught me that self-love is frivolous because it is not utilitarian. Self-love can't be monetized and doesn't increase productivity, so I have been told it is worthless. Self-love is revolutionary because it is, in a sense, a hedonistic pursuit of pleasure for pleasure's sake, for nobody but yourself. And that story makes me want to do a deep dive into self-love instead of treating it like a chore.

I can uncover my shame, see that it is not rational, and let it go. Instead of being ashamed, I can be so proud of what I used to hide and resist that I talk about it in a self-help book. I am proud of who I am, including my temper tantrums and my anxieties, and my resistance to sappy sweet self-love. Because I see myself clearly, I can choose the path that is best for me. Not the one that is just ok, but the one that brings more love and joy into my life.

So what's at risk if I let this new pattern go and if I listen to my old resistance? The sleep or not-to-sleep question only has one outcome for my cousins. I am not so lucky—I have no guarantee for a happy ending. That feels reassuring to me because to say anything else would be dishonest. The truth is I am at risk of living a boring, sad life, where I just kind of like myself, where I hide all the most unique parts of myself under a weepy exterior for fear of being too proud. Instead, I am going to live the life I want, the one where I go out and howl at the moon with every part of myself. Will you join me?

Weekly Exercise

- What are the seven dates or activities you truly, genuinely wish a lover would take you on? (Hint, hint: self-love can also mean some wild masturbation. Sending yourself flowers at work. Impulsively driving to a beautiful lookout to watch the sunset. Making a really nice dessert and eating it all while listening to the Beach Boys.)
- Do these activities alone or for yourself for the next seven days.
- At the end of the week, take some time to write about what felt different this week and consider where you still feel resistant to self-love.

UNCONDITIONAL LOVE

Self-Love Through Forgiveness

By: Glenda Smith Walters

Story:

"When someone touches your life... acknowledge you have drawn them to you... to be your teacher. They have come to help you grow in self-love and in spirit. Accept the lesson you need to learn so that the same lesson will not present itself again ."
... Author of "This Place That I Go"... Glenda Smith Walters, Empath & Spiritual Life Coach

I grew up with a father who was either working or playing golf. He played the game two to three times a week to escape the stresses of work. My mother worked full-time and struggled to raise three children. Due to deep wounds from her childhood, she unknowingly made embarrassing remarks and chipped away at my self-worth. We were never held or told we were loved, so I could only envision the perfect family setting. Over time, I realized my parents did the best they knew how due to their own backgrounds.

I became a woman of self-doubt, believing only what I was told about myself. Thus, began my quest to look for the movie version of "Mr. Goodbar" to make me feel complete. Without being aware of it, I drew men with low self-esteem into my life, those whose baggage came with unaddressed anger.

My parents had divorced by the time Sam came along. He was the image of the "Winston Man" of the '70s. I'm speaking of the stunning, dark-haired, brown-eyed guy with a mustache who showed up on billboards across the country. His lack of self-love proved to be the downfall of his health and our marriage. Sadly, this also caused him to create a self-centered life around his good looks and material possessions. For him to feel better about himself, he would find someone's flaws and point it out in a joking manner. And yet, he had this big heart and was there if anyone needed help. It took a Life Coach to point out it was not personal, that he pointed out other's flaws to build up his own self-esteem. But it was personal to the person who was enduring it.

After dating for a year, Sam challenged me by saying, "Marry me, or I'm gone." I reluctantly said, "Yes" and we were soon married—Sam at twenty-six and me at twenty. Due to poverty and his father's abuse and philandering, Sam had no positive role model. He stepped up at an early age to be the "father figure" to his siblings. He was never physically abusive, but his words and actions cut like a knife. He knew only to tell me that he loved me and often gave expensive gifts, all the while withholding his time from me.

He went through phases of bass fishing, tying flies, and training horses. He took expensive trips around the world with his friends. I became accustomed to somewhat living alone. In the evenings, one would find Sam and me sitting at opposite ends of our leather sectional watching TV. And on other evenings, he would be training horses until midnight.

By 2002, diabetes set in and Sam had a mild stroke at fifty-two. I left in 2004, with Sam showing no signs of becoming a team player or placing God first in his life. Unfortunately, his doctors failed to put him on high blood pressure medicine, so his health began to fail. I came back in 2008 to oversee his care. There were hospital stays and rotating sitters for over thirteen years.

The last two years required him to live in a nursing home setting. In 2016 his health began to decline once again, but we continued to take day trips, and I visited often. It was only until Sam slowly succumbed to the ravages of diabetes and Parkinson's, that we began our journey in self-love.

Sam never complained, and through this long process of learning to love and forgive himself, he became humble. We expressed forgiveness, as Sam showed signs of remorse for how he had lived his life. I began to see how my childhood—along with Sam causing me to second guess myself—had contributed to how I viewed myself. Slowly, I started to see a strong, confident woman staring back at me in the mirror.

As I write this, Sam has recently crossed over. We knew one another for over forty-one years. In the end, he taught me independence, along with encouraging my father to express his love for me. I no longer grieve over the marriage we could have had. Instead, I embrace the lessons of self-love and forgiveness that he taught me. Sam showed me the importance of living in the moment while leaving the past behind. In looking back, I discovered Sam had been one of my many teachers.

After pleading in the courts of heaven and with deacons laying hands on Sam, I had a vision that revealed his miracle was waiting for him on the other side. In the vision, I was viewing the back of a car parked upward on a hill. My sister was standing in front of the opened passenger door. When she stepped in and closed the door, there stood Sam looking handsome in a highly decorated military uniform. He was wearing a big smile and appeared to be in his thirties. I interpreted this to mean Sam was going on a heavenly trip. The uniform with the medals represented the sacrifices made and acts of kindness Sam had shown others.

Through this process of understanding and forgiveness, Sam not only taught me self-love, but he taught me, unconditional love, the same love God has for us all.

Weekly Exercise

Each morning stand in front of a mirror and say, "I am grateful and blessed. I am an anointed child of God. I'm wonderfully made. I love and respect myself as God loves and sees me. I forgive myself and those who have caused me harm. I love who I am becoming.

WON'T YOU LOVE MY NEIGHBOR?

Love Your Neighbor as Thyself

By: Joe Atalig

Story:

I have a favorite t-shirt. In fact, whenever I wear the shirt, you can see the evidence of how fond I am of the shirt. It's faded. It's shrunk. The neck has stretched out terribly. Yes, it's super comfortable, but I know I really love it because of what is reflected in the message on the t-shirt.

It reads:

> Love thy neighbor.
> Thy Homeless neighbor.
> Thy Muslim neighbor.
> Thy Black neighbor.
> Thy Gay neighbor.
> Thy Immigrant neighbor.
> Thy Christian neighbor.
> Thy Jewish neighbor.
> Thy Atheist neighbor.
> Thy Addicted neighbor.

At first glance, you can get the crux of this message. Love is inclusive. And....love is a choice. Yet, the t-shirt fails to clearly communicate the essence of the scripture that inspired this t-shirt design. The passage is "Love thy neighbor as thyself."

My takeaway is that before I can truly love and accept others in their uniqueness, in their differences, in their circumstances, and in their authenticity, I must *first* love myself. I realize that as I love myself, that's how I will love others. If I conditionally love myself, I will conditionally love others.

The journey that led me to a path of falling in love with who I am has taken many twists and turns, ups and downs, and unexpected curves, resulting in many occasions of feeling like things were about to go off the rails. Honestly, I wanted to get off this ride many, many times.

I grew up in a low-income neighborhood in National City, California — the first city south of San Diego. My mother had ten children total, and I am the youngest among the six surviving children. I didn't learn until the middle of grade school that my older siblings were actually my half-siblings. Their father died while serving in the military and when my parents were married, my father chose to legally adopt the children my mother brought to the marriage and gave them his last name. Because of this revelation, I began to gain an understanding of the dynamics of the relationship I had with my half-siblings, specifically my brothers.

There is no doubt that I am the "different one." I did not possess the same likes and interests as my older brothers. This set the stage for an immense amount of teasing, ridiculing and shaming. I made a decision as a young boy that I couldn't meet the expectations of the brothers I wanted desperately to accept me.

I learned early in life that the way to earn love is to be someone you're not. I learned how to be resourceful, simply to survive. I turned my fate around and began being the most friendly, helpful and over-the-top giver any of my classmates or family had ever seen. And so, the façade began.

The mask I wore was to hide behind the hurt and pain of believing that I wasn't enough. I loathed the way I looked, the way I talked, my own mannerisms, and focused on everything I lacked. But that did not stop me from winning others over. And over and over and over. I now had a reputation to uphold. Ultimately, it took its toll on me.

Fast forward 30+ years, and I had achieved massive career and financial success. I had the cars, the house, the marriage, the children and the community work. All of these external achievements brought a temporary sense of fulfillment. In life, however, the truth will always rise to the surface, and my truth was that I hated myself.

Things started to unravel. I had eight eye surgeries and ultimately lost sight in my left eye. Shortly after, I was diagnosed with Stage 5 kidney failure and went on dialysis for almost five years. During this time, I had triple bypass surgery. In searching for a kidney donor, ten potential donors were denied eligibility. My 25-year marriage ended. And recently, my employer informed me that my job had been eliminated and I was displaced. And I'm supposed to love myself?

After making a decision and taking a leap of faith, I began investing in myself. I took personal development courses and hired a life coach. I connected spiritually with the Source Power that beats my heart. But the epiphany that changed the course of how I viewed myself arrived during a conversation with my youngest daughter. During our talk, I mentioned that I want to be the fullest expression of my true self. And she asked, "Who is your true self?" I explained that after all the layers of conditioning from family and society and religion and culture are pulled back, I find my true self. Knowing I was made in the image and likeness of God, I told her that God is love; therefore I am love. Pure and simple, the essence of who I am is love. I am not what I possess. I am not my titles, degrees or accolades. And I am not what others say I am. The identities I adopted throughout my life were based on false narratives, ideologies, and judgments that genuinely did not define my essence.

That was my woke moment. I was awake to the fact that shortly after I came into this world, I began to unlearn who I truly was. This revelation caused me to forgive myself, forgive others, and most importantly provided a new lens to view myself. Today, I include myself in the list of the neighbors to love. And now I just have to make a t-shirt to express it!

Weekly Exercise

This simple activity will align your thoughts, speech, action, and energy ultimately activating the universal formula for manifestation.

When I love someone, I ensure that I look them in the eyes and tell them how I feel. I want them to really *feel* what I'm telling them. So here's a daily love ritual that will help you build a real romance with yourself.

- In the mirror, look into your own beautiful eyes (in my case, my *one* beautiful eye) and tell yourself how much you appreciate what you're doing, how you're being, and who you are.
- It could sound like this: "Joe, I appreciate how you are so willing to step out of your comfort zone to realize your highest calling. I know you've experienced a lot of heartaches, but I'm in awe of your resilience. You are so the man! You are so worthy! You are so loved! I love you so much!"
- Remember to keep your eyes fixed in the mirror at yourself, staring deep into your eyes. You are speaking to your soul. This powerful exercise will shift you in a way that needs no further explanation.

You Have an Important Meeting Today... With Yourself

How I Learned to Give More Power to My Thoughts Than to My Pain

By: Natasha Sinclair

Story:

"Here we go again," is my first thought when I wake up. I'm in my 20's, in crippling pain with no diagnosis. I have been unfit to work for the past eight months, my sick pay is running out, and every last penny is going towards alternative therapies. I am devastated.

The pain had taken over my life and was affecting everything I'd worked hard for: my career, my relationships, my hobbies, and my passions. I was terrified for my future and felt utterly hopeless. People often attempted to comfort me with veiled advice like, "there's always someone who's got it worse than you." But when you're in a time of despair, and someone tells you that others have it worse, all it does is add a feeling of guilt to your misery. There was plenty of appreciated sympathies too, but no amount of comfort could give me what I really needed: hope.

A little glimmer of hope came my way when I signed up for a few life coaching sessions for the first time: three calls over three days. I had primarily accepted my fate as a "chronic pain barer" by this point, and following counseling, psychology input, pain clinic support groups and a sufficient amount of time off work, I found myself to be in a happier place. I felt fit enough to begin a phased return back to work, and back to life—it felt. I was rather "over" trying new things to help with the pain at this point as I'd exhausted my energy and my finances. This, however, was a special "step into coaching" deal, and recognizing my own inhibitions I told myself, "if it's going to be difficult, it's only for three days."

In our sessions, I spoke to my coach about the lack of energy I really struggled with daily, of how hard it was for me to get out of bed with any sense of happiness, because of the pain and fatigue I felt every morning. I explained to my coach that, unless there was an important meeting, I would go into work at the last second because I needed to spend every last moment in bed. She let me ponder this for a bit before saying, "What if you had an important meeting with yourself?"

I immediately clung to that thought. That, to me, would be an incredible act of self-love. Someone like me who's always rushing, who struggles to feel positive about the day ahead because of the pain that hits me like a brick the minute I wake up. Someone like me, who assesses how my body feels first and lets that define the day I'm going to have. How self-loving would it be to wake up in time for an important meeting with myself; to prioritize my own time for joy much like I prioritize the time necessary for my work. To get up early just to have dedicated time to bringing joy into my morning. *Yes*, I thought. I can do this. Three days of joy.

I picked an activity I was motivated to wake up to (like laughing at the Ellen show over a leisurely breakfast, or dancing around to old-school hip-hop). I learned to rewire old thought patterns like "Oh, this feels sore," to "What can I do to make myself feel great right now?" Or "I hate my bad back" to "What friend could I call right now for a good giggle?" And low and behold, the intensity of my pain decreased—and in a pretty significant way—in just those three days.

There is nothing more powerful than the feeling of regaining control of your body, and I cried tears of joy that week. I finally felt hope that things could change. My pain isn't going to determine my future, I thought. That future is going to be determined by *me*.

Today, I wake up. I'm hit with that brick of pain I haven't felt in a while, and my first thought is "I am going to have a really important meeting with myself today." I meditate, and massage everywhere that aches. I make sure to relax for a bit before I start work. I take a long shower. I dance. I settle into work and have a productive day. I hang out with my friend and eat delicious food. I cry with laughter at random silliness with my husband. I do some gentle yoga stretches to calming music and suddenly I'm aware of how great my body feels. It's so light. The heaviness of this morning's pain is lifted. I step into my favorite yoga pose, "lounge lizard"—an epic upper body stretch where you lunge deeply and optionally cuddle into your knee. I instinctively hug myself and tell myself, "I'm so proud of you."

There is no magic wand I can wave at my pain. But in the same way aftersun takes the sting out of sunburn, reprogramming my thought patterns to self-loving ones takes the sting out of my physical pain, so I now have some pretty magical tools that I can whip out to turn my day around. It was once I learned how deeply entwined my emotions were to my pain and learned how to gain more control over this, that I slowly started to thrive again, in all those critical areas of my life that were once at the mercy of my pain levels. A sense of control and a belief that things could change because of what *I* was doing—rather than receiving another shoulder shrug from a doctor or practitioner—really meant the world to me.

Bear in mind I'm human. I don't wake up every day with the energy and spirit of Mary Poppins—my husband will vouch for that—but I do know the techniques, and I do catch myself when I'm pouring negative thoughts through my system. Learning to say kind thoughts to yourself—like I did today when I showed up for that "important meeting"s—to me, is the ultimate achievement in self-love.

Weekly Exercise

Incorporate more joy into your life three days in a row this week

1. Choose a time for your meeting

   Choose a time every day, like first thing in the morning or before you go to bed, to have that important meeting with *yourself*. Really feel into that joy. *You* are creating your future, no symptom is going to take over that; whether it be pain, stress, fatigue, anxiety, sadness. This week, *you* are more powerful. Tap into the power of *joy* this week.

2. Choose a joyful activity

   Now, if you're already an established "morning person" (steaming mug of your favorite drink, bountiful breakfast, something to read, all relaxed) then this might not be the area for you to give a little makeover, as I did. Adding joy for you might take the form of giving yourself dedicated reading time before you go to bed, or dancing with your kids before teeth brushing time. Whatever it is, make it something small and achievable (but very fun!) and something you can do for three days in a row. Three days is easy, right?

After three days, give a little thought to how good it felt to add some joy into your life every day. You might just fancy doing it all week!

Rise up in Love

Connect to the Magic of Hummingbird and the Sweet Nectar of Life

By: Amanda Hummingbird

Story:

My journey of falling in love with myself began when my 17-year relationship and marriage broke down and ultimately, came to an end. My entire life as I knew it had fallen apart.

Shortly after the separation, I discovered certain truths that led me to feel deceived and betrayed. The rejection I felt was gut-wrenching. The whole situation brought up my old story of feeling unlovable and replaceable. My heart shattered into a million pieces. It felt like my life had ended. It felt like someone had died. It felt like I had lost a part of my body. I was totally heartbroken. I felt unworthy. I felt ashamed. I felt like a failure. I felt scared. I felt guilty.

The list of self-loathing emotions I felt towards myself was endless. For a long while, getting out of bed in the morning was the biggest struggle. I felt hopeless. My body was gripped in such deep grief and pain that I literally felt like I couldn't move. I couldn't even think about tomorrow without feeling anxious and panicky.

Over the years, I had developed an addiction to recreational drugs which I felt so much shame over. I didn't really know how to go out and enjoy myself without them. I had no idea who I was and I hadn't supported myself financially for 14 years. At 42 years old, I had no idea how to start a new life on my own.

But deep down inside I had a knowing: a knowing that this was right and happening for me. It was a knowing that this was an opportunity to rise up and connect to my authentic self.

I remember the day that woke me up and urged me to begin rebuilding myself and my life. I was in bed and had barely been out of my room for a while. My daughter came over and encouraged me get up and go see a friend. When I got back later, she had gone, my house was spotless and on my freshly made bed was a note saying, "Tomorrow is a new day. I love you." I sobbed as my heart filled with love and gratitude for the beauty, compassion, and wisdom my daughter had shown me. My baby girl, now a young woman had reminded me of unconditional love and I decided at that moment to begin my journey back to loving myself. I had to for my children. I had to for myself.

It has been two years from the life I knew falling apart, to this point where I am sitting here sharing my story. In these two years, I have become a Forrest Yoga teacher, a bodyworker, a healer, and a transformational life coach. I moved and created a beautiful new home for myself and my kids. I started my own business, I met my twin flame, and most importantly I have fallen deeply in love with myself and my life. When I look back, I feel so much gratitude and so much pride for how far I've come.

So how did I do it? How did I turn my life around? First, I made a commitment that no matter what, I was going to stay in a place of love and live from my heart. I learned to stop living in the past and from repeating negative stories in my head. I learned to receive and give love unconditionally. I learned to forgive myself and everyone else involved. I learned to connect to the true authentic expression of me and be it unapologetically. I committed to leading by example and show my children that it is possible to rise above anger, resentment, and bitterness into unconditional love. I committed to living with integrity and grace. I committed to loving harder than any other negative emotion, embody and *be* love.

Secondly, I chose to take responsibility for what had happened in my life and for my own happiness, without playing into victimhood and drama anymore. I chose to be responsible for and change my behavior, habits, and stories connected to the imprints of my past that were clearly no longer serving me. I overcame my addictions to drama, behavior, and stories of a lifetime. I had to get clear and conscious of what these addictions were to catch myself, interrupt the pattern and change it.

Thirdly, I practiced visualizing how I wanted my future to look: how I wanted to feel, who I wanted to be, what I wanted to do and why I wanted to do it. I practiced and embodied how my future self would act, feel and be and made a commitment to be that person every day. I learned tools to support me in overcoming those moments when my past self would try and draw me back. Every day I practiced, committed and invested wholeheartedly into being my future self until it was more of a habit than being my past self. And when I fell from grace, I owned it, made amends, forgave myself, loved myself and started again. I chose to never give up.

I surrendered to the deeply uncomfortable and painful emotions I had repressed my whole life. I leaned right into vulnerability. I chose to rise up out of victimhood and into empowerment. I chose to embody and *feel* deep gratitude and love for every experience, not only the joyful ones. And I chose to open my heart fully and commit to living, breathing and being my future self every single day.

Weekly Exercise

1. Put on some meditation music and sit down for at least 20 minutes.
2. Begin by breathing naturally and softly. Become aware of your breath and stay with it, especially if you don't feel like it.
3. Place your awareness on your heart center.
4. Focus on feeling love and connecting to your future self in your heart.
5. Grab some paper and write down *who* you want to be and how you want to *feel* in the future.
6. Read your description of your future self out loud every day as you continue to move, breathe and speak consciously as your future self this week.

Love Doesn't Hurt. That's Attachment and Resistance

Remember, you must surrender your will to the energy that turns seeds into fruiting trees by letting it flow to you, through you, as you.

By: Carina Cariñosa

Story:

Downtown Panama City, Panama, October 2008.

I was magically called to the Hotel Veneto to speak with an African man about pink diamonds. I walked into the Casino, passing the bar full of Colombian escorts. There, I see my husband with another woman. He is completely blacked out on liquid Rivotril tranquilizers and beer. I move on to the blackjack table to greet my client staring at him through the crowd. After the meeting, I casually stroll past my husband, still at the bar, now touching the woman's ass. I touch his arm. He looks down, and then up at me. His eyes widen as he realizes he's caught, jaw dropped. Without a word, I take the escalator down, stroll out to find a taxi laughing and calling my best friend back in Texas. "I am absolved of any guilt. I'm free at last! I'm so glad he finally made it this easy to leave. I'm done."

Oh, but he would make it easier. I later received notice that my husband was 'tirado en la calle"- passed out in the street. I had to go back to drag him off the road. At that moment, I decided I had to be more selfish. I had to love and commit to myself more than I loved my husband. I realized that if I didn't respect my boundaries, then no one else would. I had gotten up to 315 pounds, miserably inflamed, drinking heavily, fighting depression and an apparent eating disorder. These were all symptoms of a self-love disorder.

For the next six months, I continued to reavow myself of the commitment to self-love through firmer boundaries. This was an extremely difficult decision because i knew my husband truly loved me, perhaps more than I loved myself, but he made the decision to leave easier with every abusive manipulation of my loyalty that followed: the extortion, the theft, the two black eyes on my birthday, the other woman he got pregnant, and the baby he never admitted was his. Cocaine, alcohol, and pills will do that to a person.

Our best friend in Panama told me of the mountain range near Costa Rica where his family was from. When I saw pictures of these gorgeous flowers everywhere, I just had to go. I moved out to a quiet little rustic cottage to heal and started a boutique tourism company. I called it 'Tranquilo House' and made a little B&B. I began hosting backpackers, couch surfers, and fed-up baby boomers from around the world.

My husband tried to follow his dreams too. He followed me to the region offering services as a tour guide. He tried to be my wingman from a distance introducing me to hostel owners while he discovered his beautiful home country and secretly stole money from his clients to feed his addiction. You see, as soon as he no longer had me to steal from, he stole from the tourists.

A year and a half later, I told my husband that I couldn't be associated with him anymore. People were thinking we were birds of a feather, and I had received an email from the biggest hostel in Panama informing me and 90 other tourism businesses that my husband stole over 400 Euro from their guests. Two days after telling my husband about that email, he overdosed.

I thought I had mourned before, but no; this was incredibly different. My ego flipped a switch as I told myself that the only person who truly knew my story was gone. I felt my story was lost that no one could possibly understand or appreciate me now because they couldn't comprehend how far I had come. Plus, I was an immigrant who was never able to secure permanent residency because my drug addict husband couldn't hold a job. And now he was dead.

Fully desperate, as my tourist visa was soon to expire, I could do nothing more than beg God's mercy and assistance as I labored through the grief. I became paranoid. I was seeing darkness in the corner of my eyes, and feeling strange, uncomfortable sensations, like panic attacks that weren't mine and hearing the cabinets and drawers slam. Turns out, he was still riding my coattails, but now as a ghost trapped in the underworld, still codependently stuck to my energy.

I began hearing him speak to me. He said he needed my help to save his trapped soul and that he couldn't leave without knowing I was okay. That's when I was guided to meet my first energetic shamen and mentors, became raw vegan, quit drinking and smoking, dropped 165 pounds, worked with ayahuasca, reached enlightenment for the first time, became a devout student of Dr. David Hawkins' work and realized I had all these supernatural gifts that I was meant to develop. That's when I dedicated my life to save anyone willing to save themselves.

Now, I practice radical self-care daily. Out of love and respect for everyone, I vowed not to have kids or remarry until I could honestly say I'd healed my deepest wounds. I analyze my own limiting beliefs and actively reprogram them rather than letting someone else's reality construct my own. I give myself permission to sleep, permission to cry, permission to step into my power, permission to reclaim my divine-human inheritance and birthright of unapologetic abundance, permission to be healed, permission to be exactly where I am, but most importantly, I give God and my guides permission to influence my path beyond my imagination.

Weekly Exercise

Remember, the energy that turns seeds into fruiting trees can't create massive miracles if you don't *will* it to flow to you, through you, as you. Repeat the following passage to yourself every morning this week and actively work to tap into the universal flow:

> "Great spirit, I allow my heart to connect with yours today and every day. I call upon the divine feminine power and allow it to flow to me, through me, as me. Thank you, thank you, thank you. I call upon the divine masculine power and allow it to flow to me, through me, as me. Thank you, thank you, thank you. I call upon me as my highest ascended self and allow you to flow to me, through me, as me today and every day. I allow this day to turn out more magical than I can imagine. And this is so. Aho!"

ALLOWING YOURSELF TO WANT THE BIG THINGS

I started to realize I was suffering from a kind of emotional anorexia.

By: Hannah Floyd

Story:

My parents and school had taught me that a good girl should focus on helping others, not wanting anything for herself. I was lucky enough to have a husband and one child, so often I told myself I shouldn't demand anything else.

The feeling was one of being stuck in an ever-tightening web. I couldn't ask for another baby because we didn't have room in our house. We couldn't get a new house because we didn't know what country we were going to be living in. And we couldn't commit to moving because my husband hadn't finished his Ph.D. I even signed up for a Master's course for my career but pulled out at the last minute because I realized that as the only driver in the family, my trips out of town would cause disruption to my son's routine. Everything had its trail of logic leading back to not taking action. This stuckness got into my body and my hamstrings started to hurt, a physical sign of my feelings of holding myself back.

I started to realize that I was suffering from a kind of emotional anorexia. Or perhaps some part of me was getting off on tempting myself with all the things I wanted, but never satisfying the itch. There are many spiritual teachings across the world which encourage us to feel that desire is an unholy thing, especially materialistic and sexual desires. But for me, suppressing my wants was unhealthy because, on a deep level, I did not feel worthy of committing to saying, "I want this."

Healing this began with meditation. My yoga teacher held a meditation class on Friday nights, and because of the difficulty of getting a babysitter I made it to just one class; but this was just enough to restart a practice that had fallen by the wayside. Now it had a different significance; it was like carving out space for myself. I set up an altar in the corner of my living room, which created a space for beauty in my home, just for me. And gradually, through my daily practice, my heart started to ignite. Indeed, I started falling in love with the people around me. I cried more easily. Even kids' cartoons could set me off.

The first *Big Thing* I was able to allow myself to follow through with was yoga teacher training. I agonized for months over which one to do. Backing up the indecision was a feeling that I wasn't good enough and the worry that I would have to leave my family for 4 weeks.

One evening at yoga I listened to a recording describing how a woman had come for a blessing of her baby from her guru and had chosen not to go back a second time. "The transmission is complete," she said. And hearing those words I burst into inconsolable tears because although I loved my yoga teacher I knew it was time to move on.

I chose to do my yoga teacher training with Ana Forrest in Berlin, an easy and cheap flight away from the UK. I was not sure it was the perfect thing, but I knew in my body that I needed a change. My son cried pitifully when I told him I was leaving. When I finally got on the plane, I wanted nothing more than to get right off again to spend the month with him... but it was too late; the doors of the aircraft were closing.

The first few days were full of self-doubt and self-loathing, but as the month progressed I started to relax. When I got back, the first thing I said to my husband was, "I want to live in a community." He could see how happy and powerful living with others had made me. I began to leapfrog from one desire to the next, learning to want the big things, no longer bottling up a lifetime's wishes. I started teaching yoga. I took up a life coaching course. We began researching the communities that existed in our area. Wanting big changes, and expressing my desire for them, created a new excitement in my family because it turned out that they wanted the same things: they just needed someone to show them what was missing.

Many of the things we want will ultimately benefit our circles of family and community. If nobody wanted anything, nothing would ever get done. It's true that liberating ourselves sets those around us free as well.

As I type this, I'm a week away from giving birth to a new baby... something I (we) hardly dared to wish for before. We're selling our house to move into a community co-housing project. To get to this point, I had to get past the obstacle of thinking that desire was wrong. In claiming and fully experiencing my desires, I learned to accept that I was not as naturally self-sacrificing as I thought I should be. I learned to love myself for being that awkward, fiery, different person who, not just content with the status quo, wants things and acts on those desires without shame.

Weekly Exercise

This exercise is designed to unlock your desires, starting with understanding where you are holding yourself back.

Part 1: Mapping your Desires

- Connect to your heart. Do so using a heart-centered meditation, a heart-opening yoga practice, or simply place your hands on your heart for a few moments with eyes closed.
- Divide your journal page into 2 columns.

- Label the left-hand column: Desire. Label the right-hand column: Conflicting Desire.
- In the Desire column, list things you want but do not have. Don't be selective.
- In the Conflicting Desire column, identify what is stopping you from getting what you desire, but don't express it as an external factor: express it as yourself having an alternative desire that is getting in the way. It's surprising how looking at your desires in this way makes you realize just how much you want, and how badly you want it.
- Here is an example:

Desire	**Conflicting Desire**
I want to have or adopt another baby.	I want to place my energy on building a career.
I want to live in a bigger house.	I want us to have a comfortable income.
I want to write a book.	I want to avoid the risk of failure, and keep the perfect unwritten book in the future.

Part 2: Choose your Path

- Leave your list for around 24 hours.
- When you come back, take a highlighter or colored pen. Circle or highlight those desires which are real, big desires: the ones that make you feel excited at the prospect of realizing them. You may find those desires on either column or even highlight on both sides. That's OK. All the desires here are valid.

- Notice where you have made excuses, and built up the significance of desires that are not truly serving you. For example, my desire "to avoid the risk of failure" is simply holding me back.
- Decide where you most want to spend your energy next. Make an action plan to turn your desires into reality.

Lost And Found

How Losing My Possessions and Finding a Minimalism Practice Kick-Started My Pursuit of Happiness

By: Barnaby Forrest Royce

Story:

My new name is Barnaby, and my story of self-love began with a tragedy. First, a little backstory. I was born a girl named Emily. Growing up I used to get bullied. I had to switch middle schools to flee from the harsh words. It wasn't until I reached high school that I revamped myself; I lost weight, started wearing makeup, tighter fitting clothes and dyed my hair. I did all the things the media showed me that defined beauty.

The bullying faded into a new form of attention. It was something entirely new for me; it was admiration. After high school, I began working as a promotional model, getting paid to be pretty while advertising products. At the time, I was in a confused phase of happiness, merely a new appreciation for a positive flip on life. Still, something was missing. Something was subconsciously unbalanced with my life. I couldn't understand my depression.

Then tragedy struck my family. In 2014, I lost my older brother to suicide. The grief led me to lose my internship, my home, several material possessions and the little structure I had in life. My brother's passing made me reflect on my own happiness. He followed the American dream structure and yet was still unhappy. I realized how unhappy I truly was, trying to live a life I believed I wanted because it was what everyone told me was ideal. Working towards goals centered around beauty, money, and materialism.

In my time of healing, I moved out to Indiana to surround myself with my acro-yoga family. There, I focused on my passion and truly began my pursuit of happiness. After attending a festival at a yoga retreat center, I found my temporary home. I moved onto the grounds with nothing more than what clothes I could fit in my duffle bag and stayed there for the remainder of the season. During most of the time spent on the grounds, I was in complete isolation. There were often days that went by when I wouldn't see a single person, With no phone or Wifi, I was completely detached from society and had no one to impress with my appearance: no posts to social media on what I was up to, no outside influence on my own thoughts. I was just living in the moment entirely.

Toward the end of the campground season, we held an event for everyone to come camp for free in exchange for help with closing the grounds down for the winter. Out of all the guests we had, two came from the east coast. They were road tripping from the east to the west coast and towards the end of closing the event, they asked if I wanted to join them along their journey. With the campgrounds closing, I had no roots, job or obligations to stay. With little hesitation, I accepted the offer.

I spent one magical month road tripping with two incredible souls, visiting several states I have never been to, meeting fascinating, brilliant people along the way. I practiced patience and gratitude for days. The experience was life-changing. I learned so much about myself along the way that I contemplated my true identity. After years of questioning it, I accepted my identity as a transgender male.

Upon my return to Illinois, I began my new journey. I started my medical transition from female to male. I shaved off my beautiful, hip-length hair, the main attachment to my femininity. It was such an incredibly liberating feeling. I shopped in the men's section for the first time. In all my life, it was the first time I identified and presented as male. I was terrified occupying male reserved spaces in the early stages. After startling a little girl in a Target bathroom, I made the decision to start using the men's room; she asked her mother why there was a boy in the girl's room. I made the switch because I would rather face my fears than incite them.

It took complete isolation and a newfound sense of self-love for me to finally begin living my true life. In my youth, I knew I was always different, unsure how to express myself at most times. At a young age, I knew nothing about being transgender or that it was even a possibility to transition. Not until I was out of high school did I learn of the process. At that point in life, I wasn't ready to face the ridicule, rejection or ostracism. I wasn't strong enough to return to the bullying. Growing up, my big brother was my protector. He taught me how to be strong through all of it. In a way, he still does. I like to think that because of him, I was strong enough to take that big step in my life.

My self-love was finding my truth and accepting myself for who I am. Not by following the media's beauty standard or stressing what society thought of me. Even when I fit that mold, I questioned why I was still so unhappy. These days I practice minimalism and take time away from social media to recharge. I use traveling and camping trips to realign my mind, revisiting that isolation method. Minimalism helps me take risks I wouldn't take out of fear of losing possessions. Now, rather than collecting materials to showcase as a symbol of success, I possess more opportunity for priceless experiences, which is my personal interpretation of ultimate wealth.

Weekly Exercise

Over the next week, carve out some time to ask yourself these questions:

- Would you pass up the opportunity to be happy because of fear or what society/family raises you to feel uncomfortable by?
- If your pursuit of happiness would shift people's views of you away from the "norm," would you continue to pursue it?
- When you cut out appearance, money and reputation, what is your idea of success? Worth? Wealth?
- If no one was around to change the impression of, would you still be making the life decisions you are now?

I want you to plan a solo trip. It can be anywhere, anytime and any duration. During that trip, disconnect from social media. Don't even take a photo. Be there in the moment. Study your surroundings and your emotions. What brought you there if it wasn't to show everyone else online? Step out of your comfort zone while on that trip. What have you always wanted to try but were always afraid of what people would think? Remember, you are a stranger on this trip so judgment won't last or follow.

And don't forget, you are beautiful.

MALACHITE CEILINGS

My new mended heart, laced with gold, evoked newfound confidence that fed the flames of my soul.

By: Nichole Logan

Story:

Self-love wasn't always a part of my vocabulary. I thought barricading and isolating myself were acts of self-love. I thought it was supposed to look like me shutting everyone out. If I never let anyone in then I would never get hurt. Plus, protecting yourself is the most significant act of love, isn't it? In hopes of blocking others out, I subconsciously built a wall up around my heart.

A really, really deep wall that I later found out through an energetic healing session was 35 feet deep and made out of malachite. Malachite is a crystal that is used to heal and draw out negative energy, specifically with past trauma and emotional patterns related to the heart. Ironically, malachite was the very first crystal I had ever bought myself and was the catalyst of my healing journey.

The walls around my heart were rooted in growing up in a very chaotic household, where there was a constant state of conflict and tension that brought with it a lot of pain. After an explosive few years and a rather messy divorce, my father ended up leaving us for another woman. As a child, I had absolutely no idea how to process this; I felt betrayed and abandoned. I felt my heart shatter into a million pieces and instead of allowing myself to feel that pain, I shoved it deep down inside of me, suppressing it. I built walls up around my shattered heart so that no one could ever hurt me like that again.

Over the years, these trapped emotions manifested into my life in many nasty, self-deprecating ways. I was constantly defining my self-worth through the opinions of others and searched for love in everybody else but myself. I had an extremely hard time being vulnerable with men and opening up and allowing myself to be seen in front of them. The voices in my head seemed to be playing on a broken record, saying things like, "You're not good enough, don't even bother trying" or, "You are not loveable, you don't deserve love," and of course, "You are better off alone, you don't need anyone." For 24 years, I was holding myself back by allowing these voices to rule my life.

I decided to take the leap and trust in myself for once, during a four-day transformational event in Berlin. I had come to this event to make an incredible change in my life. It was my opportunity to step into my higher self, and I was ready to take full advantage of it. The first day we were told to choose partners and I got this acute pang inside of me that told me to look up; there, my partner was standing directly across the circle from me. We locked eyes for a while, and something inside of me knew that no matter what the rules were for choosing partners, he was going to be mine.

I was terrified; I knew that over the next four days I would have to step into some serious vulnerability. I took a deep breath and charged directly towards this adorable guy to ask him to be my partner. I embraced the vulnerability and explained to him why I wanted him as my partner, and he pleasantly accepted. This was the first sign I received that showed the reward of practicing self-love and going after what I want without fear of rejection.

I quickly learned a lot about myself as he was a brilliant mirror of all my limiting beliefs and insecurities. I stepped further and further into self-love and continued to allow myself to be more and more vulnerable with my partner. We were sharing stories one day over lunch when I decided to show him the crystals I had brought with me that day. I happened to have my piece of Malachite, and I told him the story about it and how it was the very material that I had built up around my heart. He held the crystal in his hand and acknowledged that it felt heavy, he asked me if I wanted to get rid of it and that was when my heart sank. I sat there thinking about how this was the worst yet also the best idea. If I really wanted to knock down those walls, I needed to take action.

I was giddy with nerves but decided to take the leap and fully trust in myself. I gave him the crystal, which he later released through a special ceremony during the transformational event. As I relinquished the metaphorical keystone that held the walls together around my heart, I felt a warmth in the center of my chest like never before. For the first time in my life, I knew that regardless of what happens, I am the physical existence of love. I loved myself enough to erase my fear of rejection altogether.

I continued to pour self-love into my heart by allowing myself to be fully vulnerable and love myself fiercely and unwaveringly through each moment. Self-love is loving yourself because of your flaws and your darkness and feeling confident in the fact that your needs and wants are just as critical as everyone else's. The more I practiced acts of self-love, the more I could feel the cracks in my heart beginning to mend. I imagined it like the ancient Japanese art known as Kintsugi; a centuries-old practice of fixing broken pottery with gold. Rather than throwing away the broken bowl or cup, they celebrate each artifact's unique history by emphasizing its fractures and breaks. Just like the ancient Japanese tea bowls, I was beginning to repair myself with beautiful golden light, revitalizing it with new life.

My new mended heart, laced with gold, evoked newfound confidence that fed the flames of my soul. I was experiencing, for the first time, a profound connection with my inner truth. The simple act of loving myself unconditionally allowed for me to express my wants and needs as the brazen self-love warrior I have become. Opening up and showering yourself in self-love exposes you to an entirely new world. Your perspective is expanded, and you can see past your limiting beliefs and doubts.

Weekly Exercise

Self-love is the practice of unconditionally loving yourself regardless of the situation. To unconditionally love ourselves, we first need to forgive ourselves for all the things we have held onto or punished ourselves for. Use this forgiveness ceremony to mend your relationship with your past selves.

Repeat daily for an entire week and call forth a different past self each time you sit down.

1. Find a comfortable, seated position. Close your eyes and turn on your breath. Inhale through the nose and exhale out of the mouth. On the exhale, relax.
2. Call a version of your past-self forward.
3. Imagine your past self is sitting directly across from you. Picture an energetic cord connecting your third-eyes. As you gaze at your past self in the eyes, tell them what they need to hear, tell them that you love them and ask them for forgiveness. Allow yourself to feel deeply and let go of any feelings of shame, anger, or guilt.
4. Once you feel like you've made peace with yourself, allow the cord to dissolve, thank them and tell them they can leave now.

5. Keeping your eyes closed, allow the feeling to sink in and settle into your body. When you are ready, begin to bring your awareness back to the present and start to wiggle your fingers and toes.

Ful(fill) Your Cup

Fostering and Nourishing Self-Love Through Internal Fulfillment

By: Candace Stephens

Story:

I can remember being young and thinking the world was truly my playground. I felt like I had an endless source of energy (like most kids) bouncing around from activity to activity, sport to sport, meeting other amazing small humans along the way. It wasn't until I began school that I started to slowly pull away from this shining piece of myself.

Like most of us, social conditioning came early and forcefully. I learned how to speak correctly, sit correctly, when to ask questions, and when to be quiet. I also began to learn about my uniqueness, or how I interpreted then, my difference. As a young girl with mocha brown skin, I found myself observing and noticing how others looked different from me. And for a while, it was just observation. But it soon grew to a hyper-awareness, as I began slowly noticing and understanding that there was something special about my skin color and how others reacted to it. It didn't take long for me to learn that my looks dictated what others might think of me or cause them to make assumptions about me. As the gregarious person I was, I chose to combat this with overcompensating in my personality. I learned early how to read others and their perceptions and mold myself into someone they would appreciate and value. I felt a strong sense that I needed to be bigger than the stereotypes that circled around my melanated skin.

After years in this performative state, I began to forget the true source of my chameleon nature. I grew up and only improved my ability to reform myself for different people, groups or situations. It became a strength and a talent for me. But I never realized that this was all coming from a deep mission to show off that I wasn't connected to the negative biases that surrounded African-Americans in the community. And ultimately, I was forever chasing the approval and acclaim from others outside myself to tell me I'm good enough, to tell me that the things I do matter.

Before I knew it, I was chasing applause and appreciation. I began reaching further and further, doing some admirable things: graduating high school, then college, then going to graduate school, traveling to over fifteen countries in three years, receiving multiple illustrious job positions and kept achieving, achieving and achieving. I was on the chase for the next exciting adventure, the next achievement that I could show off and put on display for my friends and family to see that I'm doing good.

But you want to know the saddest thing? None of those incredible achievements ever came from an internal sense of pride or drive. They came from that same insecurity and longing for validation that I felt when I was a young little girl. I was trying to fill a never-ending hole. I kept thinking the next big accomplishment would be the one that proved to everyone I was great. That I was worthy. That I was enough. But I never asked myself, *really* asked myself why I was doing all of it or what I wanted out of all of it. This was when I came to the realization that I was operating out of an empty cup for over twenty years and that my body, mind, and soul was demanding that I make it a priority to fill my cup up.

We've all heard the mantra/saying/piece of advice that you can't fill from an empty cup. With this metaphor, your cup holds your energy, your spirit, your love, and your astounding uniqueness. Many people enjoy filling others' cups by way of giving love, or attention or assistance when needed, and this is admirable, of course. However, when you are trying to fill others' cups when yours only has drops of energy in it, you often experience symptoms such as fatigue, stress, feelings of being overwhelmed or overworked. And it makes complete sense because you are giving everything in your cup to others, before caring to fill your own cup first.

Well, my cup had been bone-dry for years, and I hadn't realized that all of that victorious liquid from the fantastic things I accomplished was never coming into my own cup. It was dispersed to everyone else in my life—to my friends, family and complete strangers—when I put my sense of worth in their hands, contingent on their judgments. When your sense of value, joy or even love is coming from outside yourself, you will always be tied to the external. You will ebb and flow as their love or approval ebbs and flows. Not only is it not sustainable, but it's also dangerous and a common way that many people fall into the trap of being so tightly connected to external forces, which are inherently unreliable.

After finding myself in this detrimental relationship with outside approval—which left me feeling empty, anxious and never good enough—I chose to begin the arduous, astonishingly rewarding journey of self-love. And the first stop on this journey was making sure my cup was overflowing with all the pride, love, gratification and happiness I had given away for years. I began to celebrate myself for being purely me. I noted the things I formerly disliked about my body, character, and thinking patterns and turned them into positive affirmations, repeatedly filling myself and my cup with pure love and acceptance. This was one of the most fulfilling commitments I have made, and the results that I have garnered have been remarkable.

I find myself acting out of a place of abundance and love rather than fear or desperation. I am more aware and conscious of the gifts I am giving to others, rather than giving just to give and catching that fleeting feeling of acceptance. When I actively and regularly practice filling my cup, I don't only feel fulfilled, I feel proud, loved and free. This is why I so passionately encourage everyone to energetically and intentionally focus on ful(filling) their cup because with a full cup comes plentiful self-love.

Weekly Exercise

- Think of one of the least fulfilling moments in your life. What emotions are tied to it? Jot down 4-5 emotions connected to this memory:
    - Why was it so unfulfilling? What did it strip from you?
    - Was this moment derived from an internal want or an external validation?
    - List two or three activities that are typically part of your week where you feel stripped or tied to external circumstances for internal fulfillment.
    - List two or three ways you can avoid these or reduce your tie to these activities and practice this throughout the week.
- Think of one of the most fulfilling experience in your life. What emotions are tied to it? Jot down 4-5 emotions you associate with this memory:
    - What made this memory or situation so fulfilling?
    - Were you fulfilled based on your own wants and wishes, or based on an external promise of validation?

    - Think of two or three activities that give you these same emotions. Write them down and seek to uncover why they give you these emotions. Remember to think: Is it coming from in- internal or external validation?

- Now for the next week, commit to doing three activities for yourself that will fill your cup. Journal after you complete these and write down what you did, the emotions connected to it, and how it fulfilled you internally.

REMINDER: When you feel full after performing and participating in these activities throughout the week, don't be so quick to run and dump that wonderful internal love into someone else's cup. This week, keep it to yourself. Only until your cup is overflowing can you give that love to others.

At the end of the week, see how your sense of connection to yourself has changed. Notice what it feels like to fill your own cup and be in total control of your happiness through fostering this love for yourself.

Connect to your Core Self

Let Go of the Bullshit and Reconnect to Loving Yourself

By: Kelly Seibert

Story:

I believe the capacity for self-love is something we un-learn throughout our lifetime. Because when I think of four-year-old, preschool-age Kelly, I see a joyful little girl with a huge goofy grin, excited about life and so full of passion. I know she understood how to love herself unconditionally; she didn't know anything different yet.

Some people can point to a specific event or person as the catalyst for the un-learning of self-love. I can only point to small memories. The subtle and seemingly insignificant moments when other children taught me to question my passions and dislike the things that brought me joy. I came to believe in an alternate reality where being smart and eager to learn was synonymous with being conceited. Where I shouldn't enjoy things like singing and giggling loudly. Where I was ugly and unlikeable. I detached from myself. I un-learned how to love myself because I un-learned my *self*.

Instead, I learned to become an expert people-pleaser and an expert at becoming invisible. Seeing as I had already lost my *self*, it was easy to transform depending on the situation. Instead of learning simply for the love of it, I became a perfectionist. I did exactly what was expected to earn top grades and only tried things I knew I would be good at. I helped people with their homework, exchanging my knowledge for a few moments of feeling that another kid needed me for something or, just maybe, even liked me.

I became really good at listening. This helped me gather intel about how I could change to fit in better. And I also realized that if I was good at listening to the thoughts and emotions of others, I could form relationships without actually having to share any of my own. These habits continued into my adult and professional life. I chose jobs that would simultaneously please and impress people and allow me to help others without sharing any of myself.

It worked for a while. I was really good at my job. I was a teacher and my eighth-grade "babies" craved love, and I was there for them. I was well-equipped; I knew what it was like to be a young person who felt unheard and unimportant, and I knew how to listen.

So I listened. And as I did, I dug out their amazing qualities and strengths, then wiped away the dust of self-doubt and the rusty expectations of others to reveal their underlying potential. I helped them discover what they really loved. I helped them to believe in themselves, to move confidently towards goals that had previously seemed out of reach and to see their inherent, beautiful worth. And this served as a wonderful stand-in for the much harder work of doing those things for myself.

Until one day, at the age of 27, I collapsed in sobs in front of 45 other women. It was my turn to answer the questions, "What do you want us to know about you?" and, "What do you not want us to know about you?" I never even got to what I didn't want anyone to know about me. "What I want you to know...is that I'm a teacher." I started crying so hard I could barely take a breath, never mind finish speaking. Well, shit, I thought. I'm no expert, but that cannot be a good sign.

Looking back, it makes sense that I broke down in that circle of women, during a seemingly small and insignificant moment. The one thing I wanted people to know about me was what I did for others. I really didn't identify with much other than my relational worth. And that had been—up until then—a pretty convenient way to ignore my own needs while still looking good to others.

At that moment, as my tears caused my well-built façade to sway, I decided that would be my last year of teaching. I needed to put that same energy and effort into myself. What do I love? What are my amazing qualities, and strengths, and unmet potential? Where is my inherent, beautiful worth?

The scariest question of all, however, has been, "If I'm not providing something to other people, what is there to love about me?" Like, if I wasn't a good listener or a good teacher or a supportive friend, who would I be? Would people still like me? The answer from others was, "yes". But I always doubted it. How could I be loveable if I didn't even know who I was underneath my relationships and service to others? For a perfectionist who tended to be pretty good at anything I tried, I had a scary realization. I wasn't very good at loving myself unconditionally.

Now, I know the conventional wisdom says that before you can love anyone else, you have to first love yourself. But I kind of think that's bullshit. I teach and love people by helping them build on their strengths. So why would teaching myself to love myself be any different?

I decided to use what I am already good at—teaching and listening. I would never echo or strengthen the self-doubts of someone I care about. So why, I wondered, would I entertain those negative, recurring thoughts in my own head?

Instead, I have learned to connect to and listen to myself with patience and compassion. In moments of self-doubt, I pause and ask myself a few questions: What am I actually feeling right now? How would I respond to a friend in a similar situation? What strengths and potential can I pinpoint and build on from here? What can I practice doing here, so that even one part of my response is more loving and kind?

Just as I had un-learned self-love, I have started to re-learn self-love. That's what small moments are for. They can be, as Dr. Brené Brown says, "the daily practice of letting go of who we think we're supposed to be, and embracing who we are." I did not transform or become a whole new person. Simply, I feel more like me than I ever remember feeling before. I am reconnecting to four-year-old, free-spirit Kelly again, and it feels incredible.

Weekly Exercise

Throughout this week, observe the situations or experiences that cause you to feel self-doubt, unworthiness, or some other version of not being good enough. Journal about them using the following prompts:

- What is your go-to response to and about yourself when these situations come up? Write these down daily to find patterns.
- Point out the strengths you can build on or the potential for learning and growth from these situations. Remember to write as if you are addressing one of your most loved friends or family members.
- Provide a loving reminder that you are important and those negative, recurring thoughts that can happen are not the whole truth; write to your four-year-old self, as if they are feeling the way you are.

Getting In The Game

How I Stopped Being a Spectator and Began Being a Player in the Game of My Life

By: Anjela Dermenjyan

Story:

I knew I was an intelligent woman, yet I couldn't figure out why I kept going back for more; why I would let someone, anyone treat me with so much disrespect and disregard. Was I a glutton for punishment? Do I not have any self-respect? Do I not love myself? I would never treat anyone like that nor would I allow anyone to treat my kids the way I allowed this man to treat me.

At this point, I had been doing three decades of self-work. I had been through a marriage that ended after two decades. I had spent years studying and researching relationships: Why do we have the need for them? What made them successful? Why didn't they work? I had been coaching and counseling others on these exact issue. Yet here I was. The question, "What's wrong with me?" kept playing in my head over and over.

For two years, I put myself through torture. Once, I went back knowing he was still not over his former girlfriend. Another time, I went back after he demonstrated how disposable I was. He had met another woman and started dating her, leaving me devastated. I even went back after seeing that he didn't have an issue being unfaithful to whomever he was with at the time. I knew he was not good for me. I knew that I wasn't being treated the way I would like to be treated, yet I couldn't stay away. I kept beating myself up for not having the strength to just walk away. There was a part of me that kept wanting this man to feel the same way I felt about him. I wanted him to want me the way I wanted him. I wanted him to be something he wasn't. And somewhere inside me, I believed that if I cared enough about him and loved him that he would eventually love himself and then me. Well, you can't love someone into loving themselves. I knew all of this, yet it felt like I couldn't stop myself. As if by some unseen string I kept getting pulled back into a very unhealthy situation over and over again, and I couldn't do anything about it. I felt ashamed, desperate, and out of control.

I knew enough to know that the only place to look for answers was within. I realized that I had a lot of knowledge about a lot of things, but not much of it was a knowing of myself. Though I had many concepts of what it is to be loved and to love yourself, I didn't actually have the life experiences to truly understand it. I didn't have the experience of how someone who loves themselves behaves in these difficult situations. I started to question every thought, feeling, and belief. Through that questioning, I discovered many surprising things about myself.

One of the most significant things I realized, was that for most of my life I never really *engaged* fully. Having had a very traumatic childhood, I decided long before I had any kind of awareness that it was safer for me to disengage and not participate. I lived primarily in my head. I accumulated a lot of knowledge and kept a safe distance, yet still felt like I was a part of life.

I saw how most of my life I had been a spectator, never a player. I just never really got in the game. I became really skilled at watching the game from the sidelines, observing and figuring who's a good player, who needs to improve in which areas, and who was just cheating. I discovered many things about the game, but I never really participated. Somehow I convinced myself that this was enough.

And here, I suddenly found myself in the game with all kinds of "mind" knowledge, but my body and my emotions were not on the same page. I was so confused because, I had so much information, yet at the same time there was this whole other area of myself that I had no connection to. It was like my head had a Masters, while my heart was in kindergarten; there was such a big disconnect. How do I get to a place of alignment? How do I connect to that part of myself that I hadn't even given a chance to ever explore before?

That is where and when my quest to connect to my heart began. As a mother, I knew what it felt like to love someone so deeply and unconditionally, but I never really applied it to myself. Not really. I never took the time to treat myself the way I do my kids. So, just like I did with my kids, I got quiet, and I listened. I listened to my heart. I meditated, read books, went on hikes. I started to notice and do the things that felt good. I started taking "should" out of my life as much as possible.

If I was tired and I didn't have it in me to make dinner, I didn't. Surprisingly, my kids were more than ok with that. They actually encouraged me to rest and take care of myself. They preferred the happy mom over the tired and irritable one much better. I realized I didn't have to do anything that didn't feel good to me. I saw that the world didn't fall apart if I didn't force myself to do things I felt I had to or needed to do. Things got better, and I felt better. I started to ask myself the question, "What would someone who loves themselves do?" I approached every decision, big or small, from this space. Then, I felt into my body, listened to what it said, and moved from that place.

Today, I find myself surrounded by people who inspire and uplift me. I find myself trying new things and getting out of my comfort zone. I am more engaged with life than I have ever been. I'll admit, at times it feels incredibly uncomfortable and even scary. However, I've never felt more alive, because I'm finally *in* the game!

Weekly Exercise

1. Make the commitment to approach EVERY decision in your day (big or small) with the question "What would someone who loves themselves do?"
2. Listen to the answer with all your senses. The answer will come in a flash as an intuition. You might see it, feel it, or just know it.
3. Take action. Follow whatever you received as your answer. If it was to go take a walk while you have a ton of stuff to do and are having a hard time prioritizing. Do that!

This is a great way to connect to that part of yourself that isn't your head. Being consistent is important. I challenge you to live with this one simple question every day. The point is for it to become a habit for you to live in alignment with self-love. When you listen to your intuition and act on it, everything that is preventing you from living the life that you want to live will be exposed.

Treat Yourself!

How I Turned Self-Hatred into Self-Love in Four Easy Steps

By: Jeremy L. Wallace

Story:

Self-love wasn't a concept that I had a lot of experience with growing up and thus, I didn't know it was something I was lacking and needed in my life. All I knew was that I was miserable and didn't like the person I saw in the mirror. I assumed that no one else did either, and I created the lies that I was not enough, I was not worthy of love, and I didn't matter. I can honestly say that I have always been my own worst enemy and I was my first real introduction to being bullied.

Where my self-hatred began, I don't really know, but as I began to struggle with my sexual orientation and gender identity, it only became worse. I didn't feel at home in my own body and would pick myself apart. I hated everything about myself and avoided being alone as I didn't enjoy my own company. I looked outside of myself for acceptance and self-worth and put my happiness in the hands of others, which I can tell you, is a sure fire way to become disappointed and hurt.

It wasn't until I began my transition from female-to-male at the age of 37, that I started to understand how critical self-love and self-acceptance is. What I have learned through therapy and life coaching, is that I was attracting people who didn't treat me well, because I didn't think I deserved it. My self-hatred spilled over and was projected onto others. Basically, I was teaching those around me how to not love me, since I didn't love myself. What has changed is my awareness of this vicious cycle of behavior and a willingness to see how I have contributed to my own self-doubt, and most importantly, that I can change it. I was beginning to see myself as worthy of love, respect, and success. And throughout this journey of transitioning into my true, authentic self, I have been able to get to know myself in ways I never imagined. Asking some huge and critical questions: "Who am I?", "Who do I want to be?" and, "What is creating the distance between those two?"

At times, the distance has been vast, yet other times, I can see the sides coming together. The journey of self-discovery and self-love is a process. What I've realized is what drives a wedge between who I am and who I want to be, is the same exact thing that brings those two together: how much love or lack of love I have for myself. When I feel a disconnect between wanting to become a more authentic version of myself and feeling like I am falling short, it's then that I see I am slipping back into old patterns of beating myself up. I am not practicing self-love.

So what do I do? Well, like I said this is a process, one of trial and error, but worth the effort. What has been the most helpful way to learn self-love is to date myself! That may sound strange, but on the road to really loving myself, I knew I needed to get to know who I am and to enjoy my own company. You know what they say, everywhere you go, there you are. At first, it felt like I was forcing myself to spend time alone, but I have grown to cherish that time and to look for new and exciting ways to explore and engage with the world, and with myself. The best way to recognize what a healthy relationship is is to experience it from within. I'm getting to know myself—what I like, what I don't like—and learning to look within for comfort rather than from others. I'm worth this attention and effort, and I am worthy of my own love.

While I was participating in the Active Volcano Coaching Program, I kept hearing, "Do the magic first!" What that means for me is that I must practice self-care and self-love first, to make myself a priority. I've found my "self-dates" to be this magic. Yes, I still stumble with self-love at times, that's a part of being human. I recognize that it is a bad habit to knock myself down, one that can be broken with diligent, systematic practice, so I get back up and keep trying. I now look forward to my one-on-one time and looking back, I can see the growth in my confidence and know that my feelings of being unlovable and unworthy were only lies, which I no longer believe. I am happy and at home in my body and can honestly look at myself in the mirror, like what I see, smile, and say, "I love you."

Weekly Exercise

Join the fun and try this exercise for yourself!

1. Write down what you think is a nice and fun date. Think of what you wish someone would do for you and then do just that. It can be awkward at first, but so are new relationships with others, initially.
2. Commit to a specific date and time, and keep it. It's really easy to cancel on yourself, but practicing self-love is about keeping this commitment, proving that you are worthy of your time and attention.
3. On the big day, approach it with a sense of wonder and excitement. Like my coach says, "I wonder what will happen next?"
4. The final step is to go out and have a good time! It's that simple. At first, we may feel self-conscious of being alone or wanting to get through the date as quickly as possible, but ask yourself, 'Is this my fear and self-doubt talking?' Remember, a comfort zone is only fear that's creating an illusion of safety to limit our growth; they are meant to be stretched and challenged.

CHECKPOINT #1

Look at you! You're doing it. You're a third of the way through your self-love journey. It's easy to just zoom through things and forget how far you've come, so we've put in these fancy little checkpoints to slow down and absorb this process.

This is your moment to look back and celebrate how far you've come, soak in all the rewards you've earned, and use it as fuel to keep going.

We also put this checkpoint here, because it's normal to get a little weary along the way of an epic journey. Your antidote to the weariness at these checkpoints is community.

There is a community of people from around the world who are deeply tapped into this process. We invite you to find them as a way to supercharge your journey.

You can find them by searching #revolutionofselflove on social media.

This community also has a digital home in the form of a facebook group, where people from all over the world, including the authors, are going through this book week by week.

Share your journey with others.

Experience the power of accountability.

Connect to the authors.

Get everything you need from our websites:

Thelittlevolcano.com
or
Therevolutionofselflove.com

Now turn to Checkpoint #1 on page ___ and fill out the questions document your journey. Then come back here and continue your journey.

LOVE YOURSELF FIRST

If you can't love yourself, how in da' hell you gonna love somebody else!

By: Christine Lil*Bear Lamothe

Story:

The beauty of life is that no matter what goes on around us, we have the power to transform it into what we truly want. *For real*!

Let me share a bit of my story: I was adopted at three months old. My birth mother was too young and had no support to keep me. My adopted family were unable to conceive due to my grandfather overworking my father as a child to the point of inguinal herniation. He was given his last rights at eight years old yet managed to live to age 64. They had adopted my older brother four years before adopting me. My old school parents were well-intentioned, and they certainly did the best they could with the tools they had acquired from their parents. It goes without saying that I am beyond eternally grateful that they adopted me and gave me everything they could.

My father felt that working nonstop was the best way to run a family. The only way to spend any time with him was to make myself handy by passing him the tools he needed to fix the car, interlock the driveway, or pouring concrete; too much to do, not enough time!

My sweet and adorable mother suffered from paranoid schizophrenia, which was left undiagnosed most of my life. As you can imagine, this created an interesting environment for a fiery Aries, rising Sagittarius with the moon in Taurus to grow up in. Part of my mother's paranoia included calling the cops to tell them that she didn't appreciate the controls they had over her body and could they please come over to force her daughter (me) to pick up her pajamas off of the floor.

I didn't know much about success and positive reinforcement because all I had ever experienced was failure. Things were chaotic at our house, and it was hard for me to manage some of life's basics. I never graduated from high school, the social environment was simply too complicated. There was a lot of yelling in my house and blame was a fun game to play: Who did this? Why did you do that? This all set up space for a very insecure teenager and young adult. I engaged in risky behavior such as seeking copious amounts of external validation from boys, recreational drug use, heavy drinking, and eventually, a binge-eating problem.

A few things happened in my teens that helped me start to unwind the tension. I met my birth mother at 16 years old, who exposed me to a more diverse world of culture, art, and holistic wellness; this really tickled my senses. Since she had struggled with a debilitating opioid addiction—which she had overcome from being inspired by the hope of reuniting with me—it made it possible for her to actually relate to me and my struggles. She taught me about essential oils, made me the most incredible milk and bubble baths, and introduced me to all of my wonderful European family, who I am still in touch with today. My relationship with my mother didn't last long, however. She has since relapsed-remitted a few times, and our relationship has collapsed. Though this has been painful, I remain grateful for what I learned about adoption dynamics and myself within all this and how the moments of struggle have truly helped me become a more compassionate human being.

Throughout my young adult life, I was a B-girl (breakdancer). I was very involved in the community and competed a lot. Through I loved the intensity of it all, I realized later that I felt pressure to be perfect, and have the ideal body.

My deep-seated insecurity led me to develop a binge-eating disorder. I reached out to countless places to help me, went to therapy and attended community programs for people with eating disorders. Maybe it's because I didn't look like I had a problem that it seemed people didn't take me seriously and I felt alone trying to combat this issue. I didn't tell anyone about it because I felt much too ashamed. These feelings lasted throughout my entire 20's.

Finally, one day, after reading *You Can Heal Your Life* by Louise Hay, something shifted. I looked in the mirror, and I said to myself for the first time ever, "This is my only body, the only person I'm going live with for the rest of my life, I have to start treating me well. I am going to love myself no matter what!" And the journey to self-love truly began!

Books much like this one, along with the tools I am sharing with you below, drastically helped me in changing my life from a rebellious, insecure, attention seeking, destructive, manipulative person to a kind, life-loving, assertive, creative, contemplative, joyous one!

It has been many years now since I chose a new path and have been unraveling and shedding layers of false self-beliefs. I embrace all aspects of myself (still a work in progress) and even see my shadow sides as gifts. The journey has been rich and challenging and very worth it! I can look at the events in my life with understanding and compassion for myself and others. As the beautiful saying goes, "Hurt people hurt people and healed people heal people."

No matter who you are or what life throws at you, we all end up needing to do our own inner work or what I call perspective shift and recalibration! I am so humbled and deeply touched that I can pass some of these on to you, dear soul-searching reader. The tools I'm about to share with you may just be some of the simplest self-love tools out there. They are timeless. This is the power of them! I still use them today and they remain an ingrained part of my day-to-day practice of self-love.

Weekly Exercise

Below you will find my 3-Step Self-Love Regimen. You can do any or all of the steps. Try them out this week and trust your intuition! The key is to be present with the process as best as possible.

1. Write positive affirmations on posted notes and post them everywhere!
2. Example: "I am safe and protected, I am surrounded in divine light, I am beautiful, I am powerful, I stand in my power with grace, I am divinely guided, all is well in my world..." Those reminders will set you up each day to love yourself and to reprogram any negative self-talk.
3. Look at yourself in the mirror and compliment yourself:
4. Use all your senses for this. Example: I, (your name), see, hear, feel and know that I am: beautiful, bright, gorgeous, sexy, loving, lovable, healthy, strong, kind, compassionate, __________, __________, __________. You can also say the ones that are on your sticky notes.
5. 3:1 Ratio: Each time you say a judgmental or negative comment to yourself or about yourself, you must give yourself three compliments. If you are truly ready to kick the self-mutilation, make it a 5:1 rule. That's what I did!

Note: What I love about these exercises is that it helped me bring awareness to the unconscious ways that you put yourself down and bring it all to your consciousness to then be mindfully released. This is how we change patterns. Adopt any or all of these approaches and watch miracles happen!

It Is Not out There

I have what? This cannot possibly be right!

By: Nancy Delia

Story:

Two of the drivers were named, 'David', my favorite male name! I must be in heaven. Why am I masked up and strapped down? Why are they masked up? Where are we going? Why am I in an ambulance? I guess I am dead.

I used to think you had to love yourself from the outside, in. You know, exercise, facials, manicures, webinars on being perfect. You get the picture. That all changed on Nov. 28, 2017, when after being sick for a month with what I mistakenly thought was the flu from hell, I was rushed by ambulance to Wake Forest Baptist Medical Center and diagnosed with Acute Lymphoblastic Leukemia B cell, PH+ at the young age of 66.

What the hell! A childhood leukemia? That was definitely not what I was expecting to hear. This blood cancer will take you down fast and so my fight began.

I didn't overreact, as a matter of fact, I underreacted. I was not really in shock. For some strange reason, I felt like this was a journey I could handle but the details of how I could handle it were very unclear as the doctors let me know that I was basically dying. Blood and fibrinogen transfusions, heavy duty chemotherapy, bone marrow biopsies, spinal taps, PICC line placement, isolation, purple latex gloves, and blue hospital masks were a few of the goodies I had to look forward to along this journey. I was told I would be staying for at least 6 weeks or until I went into remission if I was lucky.

I still wasn't freaking out. I just made a list in my head of all the things I needed in order to create a 'love chamber' in my large hospital room which had a giant picture window and my very own ventilation system. I also had a phone beside my bed that I could pick up and order room service! Somehow, I had found nirvana under these crazy circumstances.

I renamed my place the Wake Forest Ritz. I had my friends gather my favorite leggings and tops with hippie love sayings, pretty nightgowns, a large picture of my son and grandson, a large original oil painting of the beach in Pawleys Island, a collage of my horses, cats and my dog, my most powerful crystals, my essential oils and diffuser, and my computer. My dear friends set up my room for me and even painted my picture window with Christmas decorations and positive sayings.

I played the Rife Love Frequency 528 from my computer 24/7. Rife and his supporters say that all medical conditions have an electromagnetic frequency. Rife treatment works by finding the frequency of the condition. An impulse of the same frequency is then used to kill or disable diseased cells. This particular frequency is said to return human DNA to its original, perfect state. I felt immediate relief of my fear and overwhelm when I listened to this frequency and subsequently choose this frequency as my partner in achieving remission.

There I was, all ready to fight the biggest battle on this mean blood cancer that decided to choose me, of all people. Not only that, but this thing became Acute Leukemia as my chromosomes 9 and 22 decided to translocate. That is talent, baby.

"Why me?" There was no time for that thought. Let's fight like a girl! Get tough. Fight! Fight! Fight! That just wasn't me. I was not going to don the cancer uniform and fight the battle of the cells within my own body. I was not going to fight me. After all, cancer had come from within my very own body, from my own cells, specifically Chromosome 9 and 22, translocating. To fight that battle would be "waging a war" on myself.

No thank you. No military maneuvers in my hospital room.

Now understand it was not that there was no fight left in this girl, it just wasn't my style to battle. I like to feel good. I love the feeling of love. I want to feel that beautiful feeling of a cashmere blanket with the soft binding that you run across your nose and smell love. That beautiful feeling of, "It will all be ok." While I was so fortunate to have energy workers all around me to rub my feet, lay hands, provide Reiki and pray, I knew I had to find a way to love this cancer right out of my body. I had to connect with something that was foreign to me. I had to go INSIDE for self-love and I had to love every single white and red blood cell and platelet. I had to talk to my DNA and my silly, misbehaving chromosomes. So, I did. Yes, I did!

I spent the next week lying in bed having a grand party with the inside of my body. I let go of any outcomes, whatsoever. I loved myself for being so brave and courageous to take on this mission and just let it be. I floated in a tumbling sea of real love. For the first time in my life, I actually felt BLISS. The very first time!

Two weeks later, I was told by my doctors that I was in remission! The doctors exclaimed they had never had anyone go into a complete remission this quickly.

Three weeks later, I was home ready to take on a lifetime of finally loving myself from the inside, out. It has not been easy but it has been enlightening and joyful. I have cried, kicked, screamed, wanted to give up but didn't and I wrote and wrote and wrote all these deep emotions that were rising within me as fast as I could type them.

As I write this, I am still in remission. I listen to a Rife Frequency every day depending upon what underlying emotion is present each morning. Remember all emotions are important and need to sing their song. These days some of my primary emotions are joy, gratitude, and love. I love meditating and deep breathing to happy emotions. What was once a roller coaster of wild, crazy emotions has morphed into a luxurious club car on the safest railway in the world.

Never in a million years did I think a dismal diagnosis of Acute Lymphoblastic Leukemia with a PH+ translocation would give me the ride of a lifetime but also the peace and comfort of feeling in tune with all that happens in my life. It is a glorious place to be.

Weekly Exercise

So, let's love ourselves from within, shall we?

1. Go to YouTube and find a Rife Frequency that resonates with what you are working with at the moment. Here is the video I used: 528 Hz Repairs DNA & Brings Positive Transformation Solfeggio Sleep Music by Meditative Mind. (https://youtu.be/1MPRbX7ACh8 for digital version)
2. Take 7 long, slow deep breaths.
3. Visualize the feeling that is not serving you at the moment. My major feelings were fear, anxiety and overwhelm.
4. Give those feelings a voice. Hear them, hold them, and let them feel important. Listen to them. They are your inner three-year-old that hasn't been able to speak. Let him/her be heard without judgment. Sit with this for as long as it takes to let go of the outcome, of the, "what if." This may take many efforts, days, just go with it.
5. You WILL feel the shift. The feeling is what you are looking for within yourself. When you recognize it and you will, you will then understand that all feelings are not good or bad. They are just feelings and they want a voice. Give them their own special voice and the ones that have finished singing their song in your heart, allow them to leave your body lovingly.

Continue to practice in this space and soon you will become comfortable with this process.

Yes, you can love your sickness, pain, and unhappiness away.

Yes, you can!

I love you.

Journey Within—Living Inside Out

Better Than I Could Have Imagined

By: Padmavati Salvatore

Story:

"The minute I heard my first love story I started looking for you, not knowing how blind that was. Lovers don't finally meet somewhere. They're in each other all along." Rumi

When I was four, my little sister was born, and my father left our home and divorced my mother the next week. We were living in a foreign country, and this left my mother to be the sole provider for both my sister and me financially and emotionally. My father created a new family quickly which became his priority. I felt abandoned and alone, without a place of belonging or direction. I often felt unsafe, unseen, unsure of my parents' love, undeserving of attention and afraid to express my needs. I craved love and attention, learning to blend in and suppress my own needs, desires, and feelings. Somehow, I had decided that my family dissolved because of something I did, and I have felt responsible for trying to keep the peace and family connected ever since.

I was often unsuccessful, however, at controlling the chaos I found myself in, and so I decided that my needs must not matter and therefore, I must not matter. Fear of abandonment drove my life in so many unexpected ways. Sadly, before I knew it, a little girl's wrong ideas of the world had shaped so much of how I viewed my life, what happened to me, and my choices. It did not take long for me to know who I was, perhaps I never did.

When I was sixteen, I lost my virginity when I was raped by a popular guy at a party. Although I was hospitalized for my injuries, the rape was not reported by the medical team or my parents. Since the case was not discussed further or reported, and no one seemed to care about what happened to me, I thought what happened did not matter either. This was another major event that I internalized that my needs did not matter and as a result, I did not matter. I kept silent. Absorbed in shame, positive I was damaged goods because I was no longer a virgin, I broke up with the boy that I loved deeply. I did my best to pretend that what happened was not rape to the extent that I then dated the very boy who took advantage of me. I wanted so deeply to be loved, I would have done almost anything.

I continued in this way, desperate for love for the next twenty years of my life. I expected others to love me, and yet I was unable to feel the love that was offered to me. I would cling to these relationships until I was exhausted, hoping for a glimmer of self-love. I was a people-pleasing chameleon and prostituted myself in so many ways. I was willing to give anything for a taste of love and attention, including my body, mind, and spirit. When the relationship became too much, I would leave. I felt unlovable and like a failure at love.

I began struggling with PTSD and social anxiety. To compound the issue, I developed an autoimmune disease called narcolepsy. Living with a silent disability made working and supporting myself impossible. Searching to be enough, I focused on others' wants, needs, responsibilities, and as a result, lost touch with my own. This combination of issues left a series of broken relationships, and a pattern of attracting abusive people, narcissists, and addicts.

I joined a support group of peers when I was struggling in my last marriage. My husband's addiction to drugs and alcohol combined with my past trauma was a recipe for disaster. Although we loved each other, I didn't believe either of us had the skills or self-love to create a healthy relationship. In this support group, and with the help of my sponsor, I started to learn how to set boundaries and ask for what I want. When my husband relapsed for eighteen months and could not get sober, I chose to leave. I honestly felt this choice to leave saved both our lives.

Another choice I made that changed my life was starting to practice yoga and meditation. I learned to be an observer of my mind and the filters that shaped my perspectives. I learned to attune to my body and truly feel my own feelings. It really was a significant step in meeting my own needs and letting go of what others thought of me. With the implementation of this tool, I was shifting, growing, honoring myself and changing in ways that I never thought possible. Opportunities to teach and mentor other people reinforced what I was learning. I became an expert observer of my own process, gaining a profound ability for self-reflection. I started to become painfully aware that my future started with my next thought.

As my powerful observation continued, parts of me began to reveal themselves and were creating major conflicts with the healing I was experiencing. For one, I noticed an inner voice that was constantly criticizing me, urging me to strive for more, or try to improve my performance. This inner voice I titled my critical parent had a habit of shaming and berating my former, younger self. This dynamic created a need in me to be perfect in order to be loved, and it seemed the more perfect I tried to be the more unloveable I felt. Of course, I still felt unlovable because my motivation concerned manipulating someone else's feelings for me. It was still me, working and willing to change who I was to be lovable and enough. This was a pattern I knew I needed to break.

I started to heal this part of me using the self-reflection tools—that I developed with mediation—to shift my inner dialogue. I slowly became more and more aware of what the critical parent was saying and started to thank the critical parent for her observation. I also attuned deeply to the little girl, asking her what she needed to feel safe. I learned to become the parent to my little girl she had needed all along. Over time, I developed inner trust, integrity, and a more harmonious inner core. It is this intimate relationship that has been the key to developing deep self-love: providing for my own needs regardless of what others around me can provide for me. I see me, I matter to me. It's not about changing who I am, but allowing and being who I am.

The healing journey to self-love has been a slow and steady, constant choice. It required a commitment to continuous learning and growth and did not happen in one life-altering moment. Kirtan and chanting have taken that self-love to another level. Both of these exercises change our vibrational energy from the inside out. One of the most dramatic shifts came when I started to sing love songs to myself that I wished others would sing to me. I came to realize that my dream of finding someone to love me for who I am has been fulfilled; I am loving myself like no one has, or ever could. Happiness is a choice and your responsibility. It's not a thinking process but rather a feeling process in my heart. I am thankful to have now found pure joy from living life from the inside out.

Weekly Exercise

- Find a love song that moves you to tears. This should be a song that you imagine a lover would dedicate to you.
- Dedicate and sing this song to yourself. Sing it in your car or in your room. Sing it loud, or softly, whatever you need at the moment.
- Sing this song to yourself daily. Do it as often as you can or whenever you need a boost. Notice how serenading yourself affects your mood and take notes throughout the week about what emotions come up when you hear and sing your song.

HAPPILY EVER AFTER

Happiness Is a Private Affair

By: Trena Abbott

Story:

Being a young adult, new and out on your own, you have such fantastic pictures of your future. Mine looked like a fulfilling job, a loving and doting husband, a cozy two-story house with three bedrooms, and two children preferably one boy and one girl, living happily ever after. It was just perfect.

So looking to fulfill that picture, I found the guy. He was completely different from me, but he made me feel safe and definitely went out of his way to spend time with me, so I married him. Despite warnings that it wasn't the best fit and I wouldn't be married to him forever, it was one thing checked off the list. I learned how to do all of his favorite hobbies, and we spent our time together doing what "we loved."

Then I found the job. It was perfect, decent pay and benefits, secure, and closer to my family. During my interview, I was told that I shouldn't be concerned that the Director was recently walked out for mismanagement. Most people may want to consider asking more questions to understand what's really going on. However, since I was so focused on checking off the list, it never occurred to me to be concerned. Excellent, another check.

Next was the house. We were so lucky to have my mother-in-law sell us her cabin; it was cozy all right, one bedroom and all. It wasn't exactly what I envisioned, but it was only a starter home, and my husband would fix it up, so another check off the list.

Then came the children, two years apart, bouncing baby boys. The last check, the picture was complete. I was so immensely blessed, and ready to live my happily ever after or so I thought.

It started to unravel after child number one. I didn't want to be leaving my son with babysitters to keep participating in the hobbies I used to. So, I stayed home, and my husband would go and do what we used to do together, his hobbies. I was the wife waiting with supper ready whenever he decided to come home. Then came baby number two. We outgrew the house, and we were slowly outgrowing our marriage more and more.

I hated my life; my very existence was virtually unrecognizable from every picture I had ever painted for my future. I was in despair every direction I looked. Although I was in a marriage, I knew it was failing. My husband was home as little as possible; we were living like roommates who happened to sleep in the same bed. I had two amazing little children, but I was not the loving and nurturing mother that I wanted to be. I had to keep them quiet when their dad was home because they would disturb his sleep or his TV time. I was harsh and short-tempered with them because I was so miserable. I was extremely overweight and hated how I looked. Even with a smile on my face, it was clear I was dying inside. To top it all off, we were thousands of dollars in debt because, even though we were both working, only my wages were used to pay for living expenses and support the household.

Despite all the warning signs, I refused to succumb to failure. I didn't want to erase the picture that I had edited so many times. I tried harder, I pretended to be happier, I did everything I could possibly think of to make things better. I made better food, kept the house clean, asked him to join me and the kids at activities. I just couldn't figure out what was going on and where I was going wrong. I created this reality, and I was responsible for making it work. I believed that if only

I did something different I would be able to make everything better. I just had to find the right combination of thoughts, words, and actions to fix the problems that were becoming harder and harder to deny.

Since I figured I must be doing wrong, I decided I needed help and began going to counseling to learn some new strategies. The first day at counseling, I was encouraged to read *The Four Agreements* by Don Miguel Ruiz, and so began the journey that changed my life forever. I now encourage everyone to read that book. If you haven't read it, go read it. If you've read it, but it's been a while, and you don't remember it, read it again. The biggest lesson that I learned and have taken with me is not to take anything personally. Nothing that other people do is about me or because of me. This has, by far, been the most impactful and freeing form of self-love I have ever experienced.

See, what I realized is that each and every person is their own artist. I paint my picture of reality and the perfect life, but I can't paint reality for anyone else. Even if my husband and I are in the same place at the same time, we are having two separate experiences, which may be very different, and it has absolutely nothing to do with me.

I'll break down the two ways this concept freed me. First, I was released from the burden of having to be, having to do, having to say just the right thing to "make" people happy. Of course, it makes perfect sense. I was walking on eggshells, bending over backward to be the most perfect wife, friend, mom I could be, and it didn't matter. Another person's happiness is their choice and if they choose to be unhappy, no matter what you do, you can't change their unhappiness. Their experience of reality is theirs and theirs alone.

Second, I escaped the bondage and oppression of being controlled by other people's actions. Before this epiphany, I often felt offended by what people said or how they acted. My blood pressure would rise, and I would relive that interaction for hours if not days. I was awakened to the idea that something has happened to them that has influenced their behavior, and my life and attitude do not have to be impacted by their garbage. Similar to how I can't change some else's unhappiness, no one has to affect my happiness. That is my choice. I can still be me. I can still live, no matter what, happily forever after.

Weekly Exercise

For the next week, commit to keeping your nose out of everyone else's business; let them deal with themselves. You are never responsible for the actions other people take, you are only responsible for you. Give yourself permission to not take anything personally and put your life and experience as the number one priority. Trust yourself and love yourself.

If you find yourself in a situation where you feel someone may be thinking, feeling, or acting a certain way because of you or you are thinking, feeling, or acting a certain way because someone else "made" you feel upset, defeated, unsure etc.:

1. Stop your inner dialogue immediately.
2. Take a few deep breaths.
3. Say to yourself, "Thoughts, feelings, and actions are a choice. I choose how I feel, and I can not make anyone feel anything just like they do not have power over me to make me feel anything. I release myself from this suffering and take back control over my emotions."

If you need reminders, put notes in the car, on your desk, on the refrigerator, on the bathroom mirror, and beside your bed. Remember, don't take anything personally.

After Trauma: The Practice of Living

Unapologetic & Unashamed

By: Cindee Rifkin

Story:

This chapter is dedicated to every pain, joy, struggle, and triumph. I share my heart's truths unapologetically and unashamed of the pain I endured and the pain I caused. If you are reading this, there was something that guided you here. I am proud of you for listening to your inner voice and picking up this book.

Self-love is the romance of my lifetime. The feeling of belonging to myself, my body and having a safe and healthy internal dialogue has been my heart's longing. At the age of twelve, to survive childhood trauma, my Spirit and my life force left my body and survival took over. I felt my light go dark, my natural instinct dim out and my creativity and wisdom shut down. I stopped trusting and believing in myself as young girls do. Trauma held me hostage for the next nineteen years, and I would spend the next seventeen years after that seeking the light so I could heal.

The pattern of violence I endured over the course of thirty-six years became the internal imprint and map for my emotional responses to life. Because trauma is the root of all violence, I did whatever I could to survive. I was an empty shell using drinking, drugging, sex, and self-deprecation—cutting, hitting, pulling my hair out—just to feel alive amongst the living. I was manic, depressed, over-compulsive and suicidal. The truth was, what I craved was connection and love and only knew how to create isolation and abhorrence.

I stand before you unashamed and unapologetic of the pain I not only inflicted on myself but on others. This has been the pivotal piece of my self-love practice. "Hurt people hurt people," and I was hurting. I caused harm to animals, and I hurt people. I had many perpetrators, and unbeknownst to my twelve-year-old self, my once sweet demeanor turned violent, and I became the perpetrator. These words freed me, and I came to be accountable and responsible for my actions. Over time, shame, guilt, and suffering released. We all have our process, honor where you are right now; it is the perfect place to start.

Anyone reading this knows you will do anything you can to survive. Substance abuse took me places I never imagined and I did things I never thought I could. The internal storms were devouring any hope I once had. No matter what I did to numb out, it was no longer enough to dim out the pain. The pain had gotten so great it was superseding any hope I had to live. At the age of thirty-one, I came closer than ever to succeeding in my suicide attempt, which after the many psychiatric hospitals and rehabs I had visited, I knew this attempt was different. Survival kept me alive, but it didn't keep me living, and it was time to get living. The profound experience of attempting to jump off a nineteen story hotel terrace and being pushed back away from the ledge by a "gust of wind" was what I needed to get me sober and begin my own self-love revolution. We all have our own "aha" moments, and this one was mine.

The excavation of one addiction, then another and then another become part of my daily practice of self-love. I learned new methods to get my life force back in my body, which for a trauma survivor of any kind, is absolutely key. I took conscious actions to live the practices of yoga, meditation, mindfulness, prayer, deep breathing, gratitude, and compassion. For me, this was the new map that led me down the path of healing. I could feel that trauma was stored and living in my body, and I needed to get it moving.

There is no quick fix to self-love, it is like a muscle that gets stronger with each practice. Survival kept me alive, but it didn't keep me living. When we practice self-love, we create choices that weren't there before; we renew our awareness, reclaim our confidence, expand gratitude and view our beliefs from a thriving perspective. The commencement of building up my own trust, listening to the voice within and changing my inner dialogue built an essential foundation for growth and love.

As a young person, I would ask the universe questions such as: "Why am I being violated?", "Why am I being hurt?", or "Why am I hurting others?" I always felt that I was meant to suffer, to stay shameful for what I had done. I punished myself for years even into sobriety and continued to repeat trauma. It was what I knew, and it was comfortable to have constant patterns of suffering. It was then that every single thing I had been through was now part of my gifts to share with the world. I tried desperately to stay numb in any way I could because as the healing began, it was my light that was brightest, not my darkness. My light was bursting to be free again. The answers would finally be revealed. It was bigger than just me. I was not alone in this quest for healing and freedom.

For the last seventeen years, I have dedicated my life to sharing my traumas so that others can heal. My message is always the same: It is not our past that defines us, it is the healing medicine we carry with us so others can find and use theirs. We search so hard outside ourselves to find meaning in external things and collect possessions, and all along what we seek is meaningful self-loving that only each of us can provide.

So you see, I am not the story of my life, and neither are you. By acknowledging the shame, trauma, and guilt that have been a part of my past, I can now use these as tools to continue healing myself. No longer will I use my hurt to hurt others; I now choose to use my own healing to heal those who need it. And there's no shame in that.

Weekly Exercise

Breath is our life; without it, we do not exist in the flesh. Learning to use your breath as a source of food for your life is a game changer. It is also the most useful resource to regulate your nervous system which creates responses to situations without internalizing them. Breathing life into yourself is a daily healing practice to use anytime you need to recharge and recenter yourself this week:

1. Sit or lie down. Take a moment to get comfortable.
2. Simply notice your breath, and pay attention to your automatic breathing pattern.
3. Inhale slowly, feeling the inhale fully. Exhale slowly, feeling the exhale entirely.
4. Start deepening each inhale and each exhale. Extend and stretch the breath.
5. Bring awareness to the sensations in your body. How is your body feeling in the moment?
6. Witness your thoughts without judgment. Notice the thoughts, but fight the need to label or analyze them. Simply observe.

When you slow down the mind, you slow down your thoughts. Experience your nervous system go from flight or fight to rest and digest.

Everyday tap into your inner dialogue by taking time to breathe mindfully. By regulating your nervous system, you will tap into your intuition, wisdom, and creativity.

See the Beauty

Stepping out of Unhealthy Relationships and into My Power

By: Kim Marquez

Story:

I was lying on the bed feeling the emotional remnants from all the fighting that my fiancé and I had been doing. Well, it was more like I would say something that he didn't like or agree with and his temper would flare resulting in things like broken doors and the inevitable silent treatment projected towards me.

"But he's never hit me," I would say to my friends in an attempt to justify why it wasn't THAT bad. I mulled over our last conversation, involving his new tactic where he had stopped wearing his engagement ring and was leaving it out in plain sight for me to discover it. I began to question what I had done to deserve the silent treatment that was going strong for a week.

I decided to do what I had done some many times with him before: give him a peace offering. I had to carefully craft it in a way that made sure I stated my intention to get along and then deliver it as sweetly as I could. Any hint of lingering resentment or a wavering tone in my delivery was sure to get me a longer sentence of pretending we each didn't exist in the house we shared together.

I slowly rose from the bed questioning my timing and decided I could fix this. I could love him more, be nicer, and stop offering my opinion as much. I could initiate more sex, say yes to more invites to his gym, and cook more. I could let him have more space at night and not always want so much of his attention. I would trust him. And even if I didn't trust him, I would keep quiet when my doubts arose despite how many times he had cheated on me. I would quell the lump in my throat every time he got a text message or a phone call. I would stop asking him questions. He promised to be true to me and I knew I could do better as a fiancé on my end too. I had been faithful to him, but I had too many opinions. It had to be partially my fault for him acting this way, right?

I took a few deep breaths, closed my eyes, and invited the Universe into this conversation that I was about to have, almost an exact replica of the conversations I had initiated many times over the past three years. I felt confident this time that I could do it. I was going to apologize, even though he was the one who blew up at me for something minor. I was going to fully own my part, even though I was pretty sure my part was just putting up with this behavior of his for far too long. I was going to fix this so we could continue planning our wedding. This would be the apology of all apologies.

I slowly walked down the stairs trying to sense his energy when I entered the room. I saw him lying down on the couch and lovingly looked at him and thought, "I really love this man. This is the man I'm going to marry."

I sat beside him, softly placed my hand on his chest and sincerely whispered, "I really miss you and I miss us getting along. I'm sorry for everything. What do we need to do to fix this?" He transformed before me from this docile and sweet looking man to a demonized entity I didn't even recognize. His eyes got really big and he threw my hand off of him, stood up in a rage, and yelled at me with a fury I had never seen before, "You're a fucking cunt and whore! Get the fuck away from me!"

I felt so confused and hurt and couldn't understand how someone could be so cruel. I felt betrayed by my own self because I had been wrong so many times in trying to make things right with him. I defeatedly walked back up the stairs and sat down staring at the wall while time patiently waited for me.

A really clear voice came into my thoughts and asked a really simple question, "If his daughter that you have been raising with him, and who you plan to adopt, grew up to marry a man like him, would you be okay with that?" Absolutely fucking not. "Then, why are you okay with you doing so?"

I had tried to leave him a couple times before, but I inevitably would give in to his pleas and apologies and always go back. The answer was so clear to me and I knew I had to be done this time for good. This wasn't even the worst of our fights or the worst of his temper. But, it was the first time that I truly believed that I deserved better and didn't deserve to be treated with such contempt and spite, especially when I was showing him so much vulnerability and love. This was the final straw for me.

I left within a few days after that fight and even as I was moving out, he begged me to stay. He couldn't fathom how I could leave him, why I was doing this—and my favorite—how I could be abandoning the little girl we were raising together. He always knew how to use the things that meant the most to me against me, which is why I stayed for as long as I did.

This time, I decided to love myself more than him. I decided to love myself more than the hopes we had for our future, the dreams we spent a lot of time discussing, and the fact that his daughter called me mommy and truly thought I was her mom. I decided to love myself more than my desires for a partner, more than the times when things with us were really really good, more than all of the adventures we had shared, and more than whatever slice of hope I so fiercely held onto to finally be married to someone I loved.

After I left, I spent some time seeing a therapist to learn the part I played in creating all of this and spent four years being single to learn how to really love myself. Now, I attract healthy relationships into my life and if I ever doubt that the relationship is hurting more than healing, I'm easily able to end it. I'm incredibly grateful for all of my past relationships, for each one taught me the importance of loving myself deeply and entirely.

Weekly Exercise

When I left the relationship, I knew I needed something on a consistent and daily basis to help me heal. I now share with you the exercise that I did daily for over a year:

1. I made a decision that I would look for the beauty in something, the deeper and more meaningful things in even the mundane, and take a picture of it with my camera. This allowed me to get creative and stay optimistic.
2. I took at least one picture every day for over a year and shared it on my Instagram page. I allowed myself to caption each picture using raw emotions and words, which eventually softened the pain.
3. I invited others to share in my journey with me and go on photo walks and adventures looking for the beauty.

I'm currently living the life of my dreams and working as a full-time photographer and life coach. I recently shared this story with a woman who was struggling with her own self-love journey and gave her this exercise to do. Since then, I've watched her grow through her art and creatively expressing herself through her pain. I hope this exercise can help transform whatever you're going through this week or just add to your arable of self-love tools.

Take Your Body on a Ride

Imagine you were an alien exploring a human's body for the first time; how exciting would that be?

By: Theresa Schweizer

Story:

It was a warm summer day about ten years ago. I was sitting in an airplane that was making its way to the preferred altitude, right above Cape Town, South Africa. I was getting ready to jump out of this perfectly fine, working plane. I knew it was a dangerous thing to do and I had been scared to my core all the times before. However now, something else was suddenly present in me; it was a sense of calm. I trusted myself. I just knew I fucking got this. It was no tandem jump. No one else to take responsibility for me but myself. I believed in me. I knew in every cell of me it would all work out. And I took the leap.

Why am I telling you this? Well, because it was the first moving moment where I felt completely calm and sure of myself, and it still serves as a reference point for me today. A moving moment for me is when everything just feels right. You're at the right time, and right place and you feel at home in this world and in your body. Life has lots of moments I wouldn't exactly call optimal, but the ones I would describe as moving are often while I am surrounded by nature.

Nature is not judging us. It just is. Every landscape has its own charm; every flower is beautiful the way it is. And we can perceive that and cherish it. Right?

Then why are we judging ourselves so harshly? Why are we judging our bodies and wishing they were anything but what they are? Why are we comparing ourselves to strangers on Instagram instead of celebrating our uniqueness? Why can we not celebrate the way nature made us?

Our body is a wonderland that can uptake the awe of this amazing planet. Our body is the temple to make us feel whole and in unity with life. So why is there this grand disconnect with our bodies? Let me be clear on this: It's not all bubblegum and unicorns. Body hatred is a real thing. People often propose this comes from media or society, but aren't we part of the society? Don't we have the power to change this?

I was a wild child that loved to be in the forest and climb trees. My body was healthy, and I did not think about its shape often. This changed after a comment of a friend's mom about my belly at age 10. It was as if someone had finally opened my eyes to it. I stared into the mirror, and I felt it deep down; I was too fat. And soon after, my eating disorder began.

I was living the normal life, on the one hand, being social and funny and delightful. And then there was the other secret side of my life: the cynical, shameful, silent part of the movie where you are all by yourself. That part where you look into the mirror and curse and squeeze your own flesh in a hateful way and talk more cruelly to yourself than you ever would to a stranger, let alone a friend.

In 2003, my grandfather, to whom I was very close with, passed away unexpectedly. He had run his first marathon at age 65, and as a tribute to him, I enrolled for the Berlin marathon the next day following his death. The training for this run gave me an immense amount of self-esteem and trust in my body. I began to regain confidence and a love for the strength that my body carried and exhibited. The following years of my twenties brought "body peace" into my life, and I felt that I had finally healed and was mending my relationship with my physical shape.

Then I hit my mid-thirties and realized I had to start all over again to accept my body. With the wrinkles, the grey hair, the slightly loosened areas around my bum and my belly, I knew that I could train harder and harder and still, age would take its toll. I went through major issues in my private life that caused my energy levels to slowly and steadily decrease. I began to run out of the strength that I believed to be my essence. Searching for a place to turn to, I found yoga and the mat became my magic carpet refuge. To be honest, it took me some time to not skip savasana because I thought it was a waste of time, but yoga taught me the skill of becoming patient with myself as my body opened up very slowly. I couldn't toughen through this one; I had to become softer to go deeper.

After this well-needed phase of retreating onto my mat, I found the strength to go out again. One summer day I was swimming in a refreshing lake, and it dawned upon me that my body can create such good feelings and it does not matter how it looks to do so. I decided to keep creating these moments where I felt good in my body. I love to feel how I become smoother every day with this new attitude. Even an aging body can learn so many new abilities—like double under rope skipping at CrossFit—and that feels incredible.

I am grateful that I can now rest and enjoy the quiet moments: to feel the wind in my face, to hear the birds, the insects and the soothing sounds of a river. I enjoy feeling the sun on my skin. I imagine looking at myself through the eyes of someone that loves me. I started to cook and enjoy this as a nearly meditative practice.

So are you up for this revolutionary experiment of loving yourself in this body? Alright, then let's get to the door of your inner airplane of body beliefs and jump.

Weekly Exercise

This week, I encourage you to go out and move in whatever way is accessible to you. Following your activity, I welcome you to take some time to appreciate your body.

- Whether its a walk in the snow, a run through the forest, or a new yoga class you've been meaning to try out, move your body this week in a new way. Feel the sweat seeping out of your pores and feel your power. Explore the joy of taking a break after your activity and resting in your body.
- Close your eyes and touch your body as if you were an alien that touched a human's body for the first time. Explore the surfaces under your fingertips. The hills and valleys. The texture of your skin, the little hair standing up. Feel and enjoy without judgment.
- Write down the moments you had a great day in your body and ask yourself: What connects those moments? What circumstances are the ones that make you blossom? Track them down and keep creating these moments in your life.

There is no limit in self-love. It's all yours to have.

Enjoy!

ANOTHER WOMAN

Learn to Love Yourself Again After the Fallout of Betrayal

By: Eva Leigh

Story:

My head sank in my hands. I pressed my trembling fingers firmly against my swollen eyelids to prevent more tears from escaping and trickling down my red-hot cheeks. My nails had been bitten down to painful nubs, a habit which I promised myself I would overcome the year prior. My heart was racing, thumping so violently that thought it might burst through my chest. Never had I felt such a feeling of disbelief and betrayal. As I stared at the phone and silently read each romantic text message between the two of them, I couldn't help but wonder why I had not been good enough. What had I done to deserve this?

He walked into the room shortly thereafter, having arrived home just after me. As he slowly inched into the doorway and saw our torn pictures scattered all over the hardwood floor, I could see in his eyes that he knew the jig was up. My world had been shattered instantaneously and what's worse, I thought, is how could I have been so naive? The signs were there, but I had allowed another human being manipulate and lie to me to the point where I began to believe it when he told me I was crazy.

It turns out, I wasn't crazy. My intuition had pointed me towards the truth all along, however, he had a way of explaining away each suspicious behavior or inconsistency, and I let it happen by allowing love to cloud my vision. I trusted him while my head was subtly tipping me off to what the harsh reality of the situation actually was: My partner had been unfaithful. Even though he had insisted his hurtful actions had nothing to do with me and everything to do with him, this was the point where my view of myself began taking a deep nosedive. My days were consumed with thinking about the betrayal and comparing myself to the other woman. Having relocated to a new country where I had no support system and nobody to turn to, I looked to food for comfort. My weight rapidly increased in a matter of months. As I glared in the mirror at the undesirable, ugly, worthless girl I believed I was at the time, I became completely withdrawn. For ages, I couldn't bear social environments, preferring to remain alone. I had been reduced to an emotional wreck, crying every day and my relationship suffered even further because of it. In addition, I often experienced a great sense of guilt about not having the strength to walk away when I had been wronged and letting my partner's actions have such a strong negative impact on my once happy life. I was stuck at the bottom of a dark, lonely hole of contempt for myself that seemingly, I just couldn't climb out.

An old friend happened to visit me in the midst of my self-loathing. Although I hadn't been in an emotional state to accept guests, that visit was exactly what I needed. She reminded me of all my amazing qualities, telling me that she found inspiration from our talks and hoped that I would muster up the strength to change my situation. At that moment, I looked down at the delicate lettering tattooed on the inside of my forearm. "If you don't like your situation, change it. If you can't change it, leave it. It's your life." As I read the words that had meant so much to me after hearing them in the film, *The Ballad of Jack and Rose,* I remembered who I was. This was not it.

All at once, I was finished crying every day out of hurt and rejection, and was not going to waste another year being with the wrong person or thinking I wasn't good enough. I was no longer going to put my energy into making someone want me or regretting the past. I was ready to do something about it.

My journey of rediscovering self-love began there. I shifted all my energy into making *myself* happy. As difficult as it was, I moved out of the home I shared with my partner in order to get the space I needed to work on myself and heal. As I was alone in a new city, I scoured the internet and found social groups of people who were also interested in making new connections. The first meet up was the most difficult. I peeled myself out of bed while negative thoughts raced through my mind about whether or not they would like me. In the end, it didn't matter because people *did* like me, and facing my fears by putting myself in an uncomfortable situation made me like *myself*. My next step of regaining self-love was making up for the lost time that I did nothing but sulk in my own self-loathing sorrow. I began playing an instrument, participated in team sports, signed up for therapy, read a variety of books on how to better myself, went out dancing alone, traveled, created art, and made healthier food choices. I had successfully used the experience of finding out about "the other woman" to evolve myself into "another woman", *a better woman*, by transforming all the negative energy based on the actions of another person, into the positive energy of loving myself.

Weekly Exercise

Your exercise for this week is to show yourself love by redirecting negative thoughts and treating yourself to positivity and light. When negative thoughts or anxiety creep into your headspace, take a few minutes to pause and breathe. Give the bad thoughts a rest and change subject on your mind to a positive thought or happy moment that you can use once or repeatedly. If you struggle with this, it can also be useful to do an activity or chat with someone about something else. This will be your happy place. Giving yourself a simple moment to regain control of your thoughts will help you to function on a higher, more positive mental plane each day to the point where it becomes second nature.

I encourage you to make these seemingly small improvements throughout your week. It's a great segue to developing more healthy habits and improving your relationship with yourself and others along the way.

To Stand For Oneself

I understood what he meant by handing my boundaries over to others, expecting them to abide by them without me having to speak when the moment came of my boundary being crossed.

By: Angie Dahlem

Story:

I always thought of boundaries as a way of boxing off others. Something very rigid, a red light; some sort of "stay away from me" zone, unfriendly and unwelcoming. I certainly never wanted to push people away, I wanted them to like me, to be attracted to me. I never created boundaries. I stuffed my feelings down inside and never allowed this part of me to be heard. No one would know what my true feelings were. I only wanted to fit in.

This way of being carried me straight into my forties, with many years of suppressing my emotions, never really feeling or speaking what my needs were or what I didn't like.

I decided to set some boundaries for myself when I had a friendship with a gentleman. I have always gone with the flow of situations, often overriding what my comfort zone was, even if that meant being with someone intimately and not enjoying it, I had never said no even if I didn't like the way things were headed. I only wanted a friendship with this person and was thinking that perhaps he might want something more from it. I made myself extremely clear in my desires for this friendship. Voicing my needs was terrifying, my belly churned and screamed, "Don't say that! You're going to offend him!" However, I stuck with my intentions and spoke up, which felt amazing. I told him I don't want our friendship to cross over into anything physical, strictly a friendship. I said this about three times over the course of three months, repeating myself so that he was clear on my boundaries. I felt safe with that and continued opening myself up emotionally in this friendship. One day, as we were sitting talking, I had just finished telling him how I felt very comfortable in our friendship because he understood that I only wanted to be friends with him. Right then, he reached over and kissed me on the lips. Once, twice and a third time. My head started spinning, trying to grasp what was happening. "What's going on here? Why is he doing this", I thought.

He pulled away and said, "I can't believe you let me do that!" I was shocked and speechless. All I could muster to ask was, "Why did you do that? We were just talking about how I feel safe in this friendship because I was clear on my boundaries." I cried. He apologized profusely and said he was only doing it to see if I would stop him. I was so thrown off and and angry that he had deliberately done that, knowing how many times I told him I didn't want anything physical between us.

When I brought the experience up with Kit Volcano (my life coach, who I had been working with for 6 months) he said to me, "It sounds like you gave your power away." He cupped his hands together and extended them forward. "Here, these are my boundaries. You take them and manage them for me."

Click, click, click! I understood what he meant by handing my boundaries over to others, expecting them to abide by them without me having to speak when the moment came of my boundary being crossed. Although I had the courage to finally set a boundary for myself and tell the person specifically what it was, I left it in his hands to guard and act in accordance to them. When it actually came to that moment of my boundary being pushed, I didn't speak up. I let it continue. I didn't say STOP. My power, my action, is only for me. I'm the only one who will enforce my beliefs.

I have the power to stand for myself. This is one lesson that will stick with me forever. To recognize within myself that what I feel and believe *is* my power and I speak this truth from my heart.

Weekly Exercise

Do you have boundaries? Do you know what makes you feel secure in being you and what you're comfortable with? Do you speak up when these boundaries are tested?

- Suggestion: think back on situations when you felt your gut telling you—this is not ok, I don't want it to happen, I feel uncomfortable, this just isn't making any sense to me, why doesn't this not feel right to me?
- Begin to write about the situation and what about it you didn't like. A person, an environment, anything that comes to mind about your feelings in that situation.
- Once you identify what hasn't worked for you, create a boundary that will help you feel free to be you. Set your boundary into standards of your desires and if this boundary is tested be strong, speak up for yourself, stand in the truth that is you. Only you have the power to be you and live by your own creations.

TRAUMA RELEASE

I set myself free from living in a trauma loop to consciously creating my life.

By: Rosie Volcano

Story:

Trauma is a funny thing. Not humorous funny, but *odd* funny. The most important thing I've learned from working with trauma is that there is no way to compare it to someone else's. Your biggest trauma could be the time your mom forgot to turn on the nightlight and you had a nightmare, or it could be the time you saw your father die at the dinner table. A trauma is a subjective experience that impacts how you develop your personality and how you view the world. It doesn't matter how "big" or "small" it is. My own personal journey with trauma has a wide range of depth and intensity. It's how I've learned to heal and cope with it that's the important part of this story, and the part I want to share most with you. I'll start at the beginning.

As a young child, I developed a habit of recounting every major memory I had in chronological order every night before I went to sleep, like a movie. My first memory was also my first trauma. I was two months old. My mother handed me to a strange woman who took out her breast and tried to put it in my mouth. I can clearly remember the feelings of shock and betrayal. Today I can still play my entire memory movie, starting with that first scene. Throughout all my memories there was a constant overlapping voice in the background that said things like, "Don't bother your mom too much, she doesn't want you around. If you get hurt, don't tell her, just hide it. That way you won't make her sad. If someone touches you, you should be ashamed, and you should never tell your parents. In fact, keep that secret buried so deeply that you forget about it yourself."

This dialogue grew insidiously and fed on every depressing or frightening thing that occurred in my life. By the age of fourteen, it had manifested into a full-blown eating disorder enhanced by suicidal thoughts and a complete disregard for the safety of my body. I would starve myself for days then take fistfuls of whatever drug was around, then drink until I passed out. Yet, I still got straight A's, attended multiple youth groups, and went to church every Sunday.

I lived a double life for so many years. I separated my darkness from my light, not letting the two even acknowledge each other in passing as I moved from one world to the other. Eventually, I completely buried my spirit and my connection to the sacred. I found any excuse I could to abuse myself, put my life at risk, or punish my body for some imaginary reason that only made sense to me. I learned to hide these habits in ways that would appear "healthy" to the rest of the world so that I could continue this crusade of slow suicide. I would attend five or more hot yoga classes a week. I was often doing some kind of "cleanse" that was supposed to "detox" my body when in reality, it was just a more acceptable way for a woman in her mid-twenties to give into her masochistic need for self-punishment.

This all came to a head, when in the span of one year, I experienced more trauma than the previous years of my life combined. I was attacked on the street and had my jaw broken. A burglar broke into my bedroom window and took everything of value I owned. My apartment burnt down with me in it. I was raped in a foreign country where I didn't speak the language. I contracted the mono virus which turned into a year of chronic fatigue and fever relapses. I got into a relationship with a possessive alcoholic and we fought constantly. Toward the end of this year, I knew something needed to shift. It felt like the darkness that had been growing in silence was tired of hiding. I actually felt haunted.

That's when I found Forrest Yoga and my life changed forever. At the end of my first class, I felt my heart open up and a chasm of grief come spilling out and all over the classroom floor. I felt like a dam had opened and my body was releasing a lifetime of sadness and self-abuse. It would be years before I would ever acknowledge or even remember some of the darkest shit, but the process had begun and I knew it was the beginning of an epic journey of self-love. I also knew it was what I was meant to do for others. The path of the true healer was calling me, and I chose to walk it.

In the six years that have followed, my self-love journey continues to evolve every day. I find new ways to love myself and release the pain and shame of the past, but my favorite method was what I experienced in that class. It's called "Ho'Oponopono."

Weekly Exercise

Ho'Oponopono is a Hawaiian forgiveness prayer. It roughly translates to the following four phrases:

1. I'm Sorry.
2. Please Forgive Me.
3. Thank You.
4. I Love You.

To fully release the pain and trauma of your past and begin to love yourself, you must take **full** responsibility for the way you feel about your trauma. Circumstances are neutral, only **you** have the power to decide how something affects you. The most loving and empowering thing you can do for yourself is to take full responsibility for all of it and set yourself free.

- The traditional Hawaiian way to practice Ho'Oponopono is in salt water. If you don't have an ocean handy, just make an Epsom salt bath and light some candles.

- Picture the painful memory or person associated with that memory.

With each inhale, feel the emotion coming up fully, and with each exhale, say one of the above phrases. Repeat those phrases with each exhale until you feel the power of that trauma start to dissolve and wash away. Make sure you rinse off completely to cleanse yourself energetically.

- Repeat this process as many times as you need to, for as many memories as you need to.

Note: Ho'Oponopono was discovered and popularized by the book, "Zero Limits" by Dr. Joe Vitale and a native Hawaiian named Dr. Ihaleakala Hew Len. To discover and learn more about this amazing healing technique, check out the book.

28-MINUTE TRANSFORMATION

Where There is Love, The Demon Cannot Feed

By: Jambo Truong

Story:

The journey and discussions of self-love have probably been going on since our very first incarnation! Love, in general, is a topic whose definition has been desperately sought for generations, and probably will continue to be for many more to come.

I started life in Vietnam, and soon developed an eating disorder. I know self-loathing. I spent my whole life hating my extra skin, having all the "wrong" shapes, and never believing myself to be a part of anything. I am the eldest son of the eldest son, and in East Asian cultures, that means I represent the family. It was important for me to be porcelain-white and round, so I very quickly learned that eating all of my food meant I was not only valued, but the embodiment of love itself. I remember following guidelines of how to conduct myself at the dinner table. Conversely, I also remember several trips to the bathroom bringing the food back up, as young as age seven.

Eventually, I reached a point where life seemed like it should have been great on paper, but there was a stone deep inside that held the paper down from truly flying in the sky. There I was; living my life traveling the world, and loved by my co-workers. I was either single, dating, or wrapped up entirely in some karmically-unfolding romance, and getting to do exactly what I loved. But this hollow and heavy rock inside me prevented me from truly blossoming.

I tasted the fruits of many lands and sampled their traditions, but how deeply did any of this stuff really reach? Albeit experiencing so many wonders, I often questioned how much of the full flavor of life I was really getting.

The quest began a number of years ago when I decided to really unpack this matted web of complexities. As I sought a definition of love and investigated the outcomes of the lives of those who knew love, the first things that came to me were feelings of loss and confusion. Eventually, the only conclusion I could draw was that there exists a plethora of explanations and inspirations, but they all suggest that anyone can create change through their own conceptions of love.This told me that love itself can manifest in more ways than can possibly be numbered, but even after all that, I still felt like a complete beginner.

So, I started with self-compassion, mainly because at the time of my questioning there was already a great deal of research available around it. Some of the obvious factors were how acts of self-compassion lowered cortisol, and improved coherence and relationships with ourselves and others. A great start indeed! I could relate to these areas and apply self-love with such knowledge.

I would speak five wonderful things to myself every morning, and five things I was grateful to myself for doing every day. The point of this practice was to wait until they were fully felt. This offered me a fuel that would inspire me to do positive self-talk throughout the day. This juicy energy was propelling me into touching the inner surfaces of deeper self-acceptance; so much so that I then went onto discover that 'I Am Enough'.

At first, it was around recognizing that my efforts were enough, my presence was enough, and what I had was enough. This reminded me so much of my mother's Vietnamese influence; a culture that is so grateful for what they have to work with. This, in turn, offered the inner peace that is behind the smiles of many Vietnamese people. Contentment of what they have, and acceptance of what they have to work with.

Today, I believe that I am not only more than enough, but the phrase 'enough' simply isn't sufficient in describing what I, nor any of us, really are. Now, I am filled with a fullness that wants me to delve into feelings even deeper inside, because I was able to unpack the moments when I did not feel enough. More importantly, I discovered forgiveness.

Every day I chose one person to forgive (on a good day I was able to let go of many). As I sat with whomever and worked out how to forgive, I finally realized that forgiving them was far more important for myself than for them. To release the inflammation from this relationship so as not to experience it further was one of the most profound bodily experiences I'd ever had.

At the current stage of my quest to define self-love, I have realized that all the people that I've wanted to forgive also wanted to give me love in some way, shape, or form. I recognize that within me, there is a desire to control how I uptake love. Maybe this is because I associate love with being ia particular way, and when another behaves in complete opposition to how I define this ageless subject, I trigger.

Every day I sit for 28 minutes, accepting love. I go back to my earliest memories, or sometimes I use something very easy to connect to, like someone giving me a hug. 28 minutes for yourself to receive that which was always meant for you is not a lot of time. But it shifts the rest of the day. Why does it shift the rest of the day?

Imagine a child who was given all the love in the world and believed that they were loved, and compare them to a child that was not given love, or had love taken away from them. How would each one mature into the world?

After only a few months of sitting and uptaking love from my family, friends, ex-partners, teachers, students, trainees, and mentees, I have come to realize that there is an energy that is truly abundant for us—and that as much as I sit and absorb, I will probably not uptake it all in this lifetime. I feel energized, recuperated, charged up, and ready to go. I feel any heaviness that I may have picked up throughout my day, washed right out when there is the presence of love.

I have felt the resonance of addictive behaviors fall by the side when I can feel the presence of love inside. I have seen how this practice provides the lubrication for that which is stuck deep inside, to lift up to the surface and leave for good.

Where there is love, the demon cannot feed.

Weekly Exercise

- Please join me every day for 28 minutes. Set a timer, choose up to five people or animals that you wish to uptake love from.
- Choose beings who you KNOW love you. It makes the exercise much easier.
- Do not open your eyes until the timer goes off. Use whatever music and sitting position that is going to enable you to pay attention to something very important.
- After 28 minutes open your eyes and dive deep into your world with love deep inside of your core and filling the space right behind you.

Stumbling Onto Strength

How Feeling Turns into Healing

By: Lauren May

Story:

I thought I was stronger. I thought I had conquered that part of myself that loved others so much it clouded my view of common sense. I thought there was no way this could happen again. I was stronger, I was happier, I knew myself. How could this happen again?

I stormed off in a fit of rage. I was at a parade in a town twenty minutes from where I lived and I decided to be conscientious and carpool with other people. I thought a group of us were going: myself, the person I had been dating, and two other people. One person disappeared as soon as we arrived, and not long after that I realized the person I was dating brought the other person as their date and not me. I didn't anticipate the night to go as it did. I didn't anticipate being stranded, crying, on the side of a random road in an unfamiliar town. I didn't anticipate the blatant disregard for my feelings and the shots of alcohol that made the words that were exchanged feel like daggers. I couldn't wrap my head around it. I couldn't believe that the person I let myself love this much could hurt me this way and have absolutely no remorse about it. The tears began to fall and I couldn't take the situation a second longer; I stormed off. I headed in the direction to get as far away from the situation as possible. I ended up on a curb in front of an random church on a side road and I knew what I had to do—call my best friend to come rescue me.

"How could this happen again," I thought to myself. "How did I end up in another situation where I gave my heart away and was humiliated? I thought I knew better this time."

It was the longest twenty minutes of my life, sitting there on the curb. I was replaying the whole night, how it transpired, how the evening turned from a fun and new experience to my own humiliating hell. I replayed the entire last year over and over in my head and began to recognize the signs I had ignored all along the way. I wanted to blame the entire situation on someone else but my part in it couldn't be ignored. As I sat there anxiously awaiting my ride, trying to wipe the tears away, I could feel it deep in my soul that I would never be the same after this. This hurt in a big way and I needed it to never happen again.

The next few months were filled with alcohol, staying busy, and a lot of tears. Anything to distract myself from feeling. I made new friends with city locals, adopted my new motto, "feelings are the devil", and created a "singles awareness club" with a friend—in part for accountability, but mainly so I could never give my heart away and get hurt in the same way I had ever again. What started out as a way to avoid my feelings quickly turned into a way to heal them head on. With my new freedom from a relationship, I had nothing but time to spend catering to myself. I got a gym membership, joined a group workout class, I planned fun trips, I invested in friendships, I went to concerts, I stepped out of my comfort zone and allowed myself to see the full scope of beauty life had to offer. I woke up every single day with the goal of feeling less miserable than I did the day before, and before I knew it, my goal was paying off.

My workout class quickly became a mental crutch. Five days a week we would push our bodies to the extreme, and then rejoice in the sweat and muscle fatigue when the class came to an end. That workout class and those people showed me the mental strength I needed during a time I felt I had none. I found the confidence to share my new passion by taking my friends to a Kyle Cease event. I was living a life with a new level of open-mindedness that I had never experienced before, and I was loving every minute of it. I began to notice that I was making a conscious effort every day to be around people that I loved and cared about, and I was starting to feel happy again. Even with all of the other changes I made, I still took the singles awareness club seriously. I was still upholding my promise to myself, that the next time I put my heart out there it would be worth it (spoiler alert, that didn't turn out as anticipated either, but somehow I was still okay).

The first heartbreak I experienced, a dead relationship that I tried to revive for nearly seven years, the night I explained above, and even the time after that, I put my heart out there and it didn't work out—but the world continued on. Those experiences were officially a part of my past, and I had finally, truly believed it. I felt like a completely different person in those lifetimes. In those relationships, I was a victim and I let that be a defining characteristic for too long. Did my heart break? Absolutely. Did I lose people that at the time I thought were "forever"? Absolutely. But what I "lost" is incomparable to what I gained. After my self-pity alcohol binge, and the many nights I spent crying alone, I found myself. I found self-awareness and respect. I found my voice and my ability to stand up and use it. I learned that the moment I start to sacrifice the person I am in a relationship is the exact moment I need to get out of that relationship. I became aware of how essential it is to have boundaries in any relationship. I became accustomed to taking responsibility for my own actions and understanding how they can affect others. I had changed. The reflection I saw in the mirror now was unrecognizable, but for the first time in a long time, it was a pleasant kind of unrecognizable.

Now, when I look back on the entire situation that led me to the parade that night the only state of mind I go to is satisfaction. I feel satisfied knowing that I took a raw, deep, emotional time in my life and turned it into a lesson. I made it a reason to move forward and become a better person. Before I found myself crying alone on a curb, I catered to other people, I put others happiness before my own, I let people make choices for me. I let my love for other people overshadow what was best for me. I could become anything anyone wanted me to be, but I never took the time to become what I wanted for myself. I was too busy trying to make everyone else happy. The parade night, along with many other nights from my past, merged together and showed me that I could never be in another relationship that made me compromise my standards. There was no way I could give love to another person safely until I loved myself enough to stand up for *me.* Love should not mean compromising oneself, and had I not stormed off in a fit of rage that night it may have taken me a lot longer to understand that. This will never happen again because now, I am stronger, I am happier, I know myself and I love myself.

Weekly Exercise

1. Write down a quality you love about yourself but often sideline for the sake of others. Journal about how you can prevent yourself from sidelining this quality in your future relationships.

You Are Responsible For You

I viewed myself through the lens of victimhood, unable to stretch my arms without hitting someone in the process.

By: Carrie Dungey

Story:

It would seem reasonable that, after you tell your children that their father has died, you would focus and concentrate solely on their wellbeing.

As grief is generally a multi-faceted, many-layered process with no clear or predictable path, it certainly isn't one that anyone, especially a child, should ever have to walk alone. There are so many questions. There are unimaginable feelings. There is the sweet release of tears. There is the attempt to explain the story to friends and family and strangers. There is even humor to cut through the grief and help make things feel as normal as possible.

For so long, I've wanted to believe that the tragedy that turned my life and my children's' lives upside down was one of the main sources of my codependent parenting and emotional dysregulation, however I know now that I have used it as an excuse to take care of others at the expense of taking care of myself.

Following the death, I delved into reading articles and books about children and grief, and about how to talk with children about suicide and death. I talked with friends, I consulted therapists and experts in the field, I searched for grief groups for children.

I took them to art therapy every week for over a year.

I quit work to stay at home with them.

I enrolled them in horse-riding lessons.

My laser-beam, eagle-eye focus was on my daughters and almost everything I did was for them.

Less than 2 years later, I got remarried and not long after that, I found another job and started working full-time again.

With two lovely children, a dedicated and supportive husband, a full-time job—and even a new puppy—you would think that I would have been on top of the world, but instead, I was often found sobbing under the covers. I felt devoid of purpose, paralyzed by indecision, anxious about everyone and everything, and my world felt as small as the bed I continued to lie crying in.

I finally made the decision to pursue therapy again and from there, I enrolled in an 8-week mental health and wellness program that focused on becoming aware of my thoughts and the stories behind why I was thinking them. This felt healthy. For once, I was focusing on my thoughts and not the thoughts of others.

A year following that, I had my third baby and ended up being enrolled in a postpartum depression research study which included weekly group sessions that fostered even more awareness into the subconscious thoughts that can drive us so wildly all over the mental and emotional map.

There was also an intense focus on self-care, which I understood in theory but dismissed with a multitude of excuses as to why it simply wasn't possible for me. In short, I convinced myself that self-care was too difficult for me. I had no time and I had no energy. My baby was so little and was breastfeeding and I was,in my mind, unable to extricate myself from her. And, while there may be some truth to the logistics and rigors of life with a young baby, I acknowledge that I allowed myself to be overwhelmed in order to not have to take responsibility for me, for my life or for my needs and wants. I continued to give and give when I could have asked for help. I continued to give until I was exhausted and sobbing every day of my life.

My cup had emptied long ago and I continued to try and pour out what was no longer there to give.

My attempts to take care of myself were feeble and usually ended up with me feeling guilty for 'abandoning' my family and 'selfishly' focusing on myself.

I viewed myself through the lens of victimhood, unable to stretch my arms without hitting someone in the process. What I didn't understand was that, in thinking of myself as a victim, I also saw everyone around me as victims who constantly needed my rescuing.

It was when I signed up for a life coaching program that my eyes were finally opened to the idea of victim mentality and how it can play out along with its sibling, codependency. I see now that, like medicine, compassion,kindness and caring must all be given at the proper dose lest the medicine become poison. Compassion and care must also be extended to oneself before they can truly be offered to others. Caregiving must be done from a place of love and not of rescue, obligation or resentment.

This became much clearer when I woke up one morning with my mind yelling *"I am responsible for me"*. These words felt like freedom.

They did not absolve me from paying my bills, going to work or feeding my children.

"I am responsible for me" means that, if I tell myself that everyone else has more money than I do, I am responsible for being aware of this thought and bringing my thinking back in line with what I desire and not with drowning in self-pity.

"I am responsible for me" means that, if I don't take my self-care bath or a solo walk around the block, I can't point my exhausted finger at anyone but me. Neither is this done with the intention of self-incrimination but with the loving and powerful intention of seeing myself as the one who decides whether I will be depleted or lifted up.

This phrase also means that...

I am responsible for reaching out for help and support.
I am responsible for keeping in tune with my intuition and following my heart.
I am responsible for being aware of the path that my thinking and emotions are taking, and getting back on the right path for me when I make a misstep (or two or three!)
I am responsible for grieving my losses
I am responsible for apologizing and making things right when I have hurt people I love.

This has helped me see life and love from an entirely new lens.

I now see that I truly am the creator of my life. That my decisions create my destiny. That the power is fully in me to take care of myself and, in doing so, be the best version of me. I am not perfect—this lesson is still very much in progress—but I am becoming more aligned with the vision of me as a capable, self-nurturing, self-compassionate individual.

Weekly Exercise

Ask yourself if there are areas of your life where you have avoided taking responsibility. Have you found yourself depleted from overgiving to others while forgetting about yourself?

1. Take out a journal and set a timer to 10 minutes. Think of areas or specific moments in your life that you have avoided taking responsibility. List as many as you can down.
2. Reflect on each moment you came up with. What was the source of this? What emotions came up when you avoided responsibility?

3. Identify where you can take responsibility today and celebrate yourself when you do.

Taking responsibility for taking care of yourself is something that will shift almost every other aspect in your life for the better!

Breaking the Cycle of Stupidity

Seeking the approval of others used to distract me from deciphering what I want— now I am finally putting myself first.

By: Maggie Laurino

Story:

I used to think that if I paid my dues to the gods of shitty relationships, they would eventually say "okay enough hazing - here's a good guy for you!" Now, of course, I never actually believed that the world works that way. But I wanted it to. I wanted there to be a formula. *Getting ghosted by five guys gets you one month of texts back. Putting up with three boring dates earns you one promising one.* I used to joke with my friends about being the authority on this because I had built up what I call a "large sample size". It's unfortunate that studying men is not a lucrative career, because I have tons of experience analyzing their every move.

Over time, I trained myself to value other people's approval of me over my own opinions of them. I lost sight of my own voice and what I wanted. Forget about being good enough for a guy, is he good enough for me? What about me? To this day, I still battle with the part of me that wants to be reckless and put men on a pedestal. But I want to talk about the proverbial angel on my shoulder. The strong, independent woman who *"don't need no man"*. How can I make sure that she's always in charge?

About a year ago, I was broken up with in a Panera Bread parking lot. Now, every time I go to that Panera, I think about how much of a mess I was - sobbing loudly, and dramatically exiting my boyfriend's car to go cry in my own car. I mean, who does that? After overcoming the trauma of a parking lot breakup, I stuck my toes into the tepid waters of the dating scene. I resumed my formulaic approach.

Step 1: Endure shitty behavior from a stupid boy.
Step 2: Continue to see him.
Step 3: Text him first - don't wait for him to! He's probably not texting you because he's waiting for you to do it!
Step 4: Complain about his lack of commitment, and dramatically call him out.
Step 5: End all contact.
Step 6: Drunk text him at 2AM.
Rinse and repeat.

Well, if doing the same thing and expecting a different result is the definition of insanity, then I'm probably insane. But when you're slightly insane and majorly tenacious like me, you keep trying.

A few weeks ago I was on Step 4 for probably the second or third time with this guy - complaining about his shortcomings (that I saw when we first met). Here I am getting heated, having fun with telling him I'm annoyed when he says, "You always say that. But you keep hanging out with me".

Okay, whoa. First of all, I'm mad because I don't like to be wrong. I hated how right he was. I was on my high horse and he just toppled it right over. So being me, I repeated Steps 1 and 2, and spent the night with him for the first time. And the last time. I left the next morning and felt like a walking cliché. In the bright sun of a fall Philly morning— my clothes smelling like a smoky all-male apartment—things became a bit clearer. This whole thing with this guy had gone way too far. I had never spent a night before work at someone else's place, and I could feel the anger pulsing through my hands as I drove home. I kept asking myself, *"How did I get here? How did I let him take away my control like this?"* I felt like I was losing myself - throwing myself into a pseudo-relationship that I literally knew was destined to fail. On top of his warning that he didn't want anything serious, he was a walking red flag.

I was so frustrated with myself, and I couldn't ignore the small voice in my head that was always there, waiting for things to go wrong. I finally had to admit to myself that my cycle of self-abuse wasn't working. In seeking love, I was attracting everything but love. I told Step 4 Guy that I could not continue seeing him, because I felt like my need for emotional availability wasn't something he could fill. This was a win for me. I knew that time was legit.

The one part of my cycle of stupidity that I didn't mention is the last part, where I leave things open-ended, for a long time. With Panera-parking-lot-breakup boy, Step 4 Guy, and a mess of other guys who have been in my life, I've never quite gotten the hang of the firm goodbye. The times that things have ended; I've left a door open for these people to re-enter my life. Closing these doors might be the hardest thing I will have to do since I've fought myself to keep them open for years. This will be the true test for me in the weeks and months to come as I continue to work on self-love. I have to get comfortable with letting go of a possible future with one person, in favor of myself.

So far, I've embraced self love in small doses, one step at a time. I continuously practice asking myself to stop and think, "*What do I want?*" Whether it's a career move, plans for a Friday evening, or whether or not to go to an Eagles football game on a Monday night, I'm thinking about *me*. When a decision seems murky, I try to leave it to the inner voice in the back of my head: "Hmm, this job doesn't feel like the right one," "Just stay in and relax tonight" , or "GO to the game!"

Similar to those detrimental relationships with partners, I've been in one with my career. Recently, after 2.5 years working at the same company, I found myself feeling like I wasn't the one steering the ship. Before my last job change within the company, I ignored a voice in my head that kept saying *"Maggie, are you really going to be happy as a supervisor? Is this the right move right now?"* I was afraid to let an opportunity pass me by, like my hesitation to let go of the possibility of a future with bad men. I forgot that even if my team of mentors had my best interest at heart, my own instinct trumps all of that. After six months in that new position, I was extremely unhappy. I had let myself down by drowning out that voice. In doing so, I reinforced the lesson that I need to listen to my inner voice when it's speaking.

Now, I am no master of self love. But I have taken small lessons from each misstep along my journey. I'm turning up the volume on that voice inside me and doing things for me, and it feels fucking great.

Weekly Exercise

In my own journey, I've evaluated how I form and assess relationships in my life. I've examined which relationships are healthy, and which ones are not. This week, I want you to do the same. When you start your week, take a pen and paper and write. Reflect on the following, choosing one solid relationship in your life, and one negative or detrimental relationship (romantic, friendship, or otherwise).

- How did this relationship begin?
- What effect does this relationship have on me?
- How do I feel when I am with this person?
- What allowances have I given this person, if any? (i.e.: have I strayed from myself for this person?)
- How would my life be different if this person were not in it anymore?

When you have reflected for at least 5-10 minutes on each of the two relationships you've identified, start a new page. This will be dedicated to future relationships. Throughout the week, add to this page, with the help of the following guiding thoughts. At the end of the week, you should be left with a guide for yourself based on your needs in relationships. Reflect on the following:

- What qualities in a person show me that I want to be their friend?
- What red flags tend to slip by me, proving to be warning signs later on?
- What things do I absolutely need in all relationships?
- What qualities about myself am I not willing to sacrifice for others?

From Addiction to Awareness

Are you numbing out to vital emotional information?

By: Lola Rephann

Story:

From an early age, I learned how to use external agents to anesthetize my true feelings.
The first time I tried marijuana I was in 7th grade, with my friend Sarah. Sarah lived on a horse farm. She was 12 going on 29, lived with her grandmother, half-sister, and some assorted ranch hands. Sarah knew where her half-sister's pot supply was, and pilfered from it regularly. One day, Sarah asked me if I wanted to smoke. Although I had never thought about trying pot, and didn't even know much about it, I said yes.

She rolled a joint. We went outside near the horses. She took the first puff then passed it to me.

"Inhale, but don't exhale right away. Hold it in."

I did what she told me to do. I coughed hard. She laughed.

"It's okay, it gets better. Try again."

That was a night of many firsts: my first joint, my first cigarettes, my first time watching Purple Rain, and my first experience trading in everyday reality for altered reality.

During high school, I swapped drugs for starving myself. I was a textbook anorexic: high achieving, controlling, regimented, and self-loathing. I woke at 5am every day to read the New York Times from the night before. I exercised obsessively and took my measurements every Saturday. When I began college at an elite institution in New York City, instead of punishing myself through calorie restriction, I threw myself into study, work, and achievement. By junior year, I added yet another creative method of disassociating from my true self: I became involved in identity politics and protesting.

Due to various factors, not least of which was my parents' divorce, my father's abrupt departure from my life, and his subsequent emotional abuse, I learned that things happened to me, and I needed to protect myself from the vagaries of life. In this worldview, there was no space for feeling confusion, fear, or vulnerability.

As my political profile in college grew, I got involved in student government and organized conferences, parties, speeches, meetings, and charity events. One of these was the Valentine's Day Date Auction to raise money for a children's charity. It seems so politically incorrect now, and it's amazing we even did it, but times were different then. A friend of mine won a date with me.

The night for our date came. I had just taken a shower and was wearing a fuzzy pink Victoria's Secret bathrobe. A knock at my door. I opened it. A guy who didn't attend my school but was friends with some of my classmates stood outside. We'd been hooking up at parties for student groups I was active in.

I told him I didn't have much time. Here the memories get spotty. I remember him kissing me, the belt on my robe getting loose. I fell back onto my bed, landing on the edge of the mattress. I was still in my robe. Searing hot pain and sweat. His penis went in the other opening, hard. I screamed. He left. Instead of taking care of myself, I hurried up to get ready to go on the winning date, ever dutiful, and drank myself into oblivion because it hurt so much to sit on my violated anus.

Depression, self-hatred, and alcohol and drug abuse blossomed soon after. Christmas Eve of my senior year in college. It was cold and rainy. I was in my dorm room alone with a blunt, a pack of Marlboro Lights, and a 40 oz. of Olde

English. I'd decided not to go home for the holiday because I had too much work to do, a new addiction which I would perfect in my 30s and 40s: Workaholism.

As I got further away from my feelings, my life seemed to take on a course of its own. I was in the passenger seat. The unholy trinity of marijuana, alcohol, and cigarettes were in the driver's seat. It took 20 years after that lonely Christmas Eve for me to get tired of being tired, sick of being sick, and angry that I was so angry.

During my first yoga teacher training in 2010, my teacher made explicit rules: no alcohol, no drugs, no coffee, no sex. It was the first time I'd been asked to look at my habits and question whether they were supporting the life I wanted to live. I adhered to her rules, but once the training was over, so was my abstinence.

A break-up, a fire in an apartment where I was staying, losing a job and losing one of my best friends took me into a period of compulsive indulgence. I'd spent countless nights tearing through cigarettes, weed, and booze, waking up the next day with no voice, no memory, and the stale stench of nightclub all over my apartment.

A few years into this, I discovered Forrest Yoga. My teacher, Ana Forrest, was a recovered addict who'd started her drug and alcohol journey when she was just a child. I'd read her book Fierce Medicine and I had seen myself reflected in her story. I signed up for the Forrest Yoga Teacher Training in 2014.

At the halfway point of the training, the trainees undergo a shamanic journey called the Death Meditation. That night, out to dinner with my family, I got wasted on one glass of wine and still decided to have two more. I tried to hide my intoxication from my mom when I got up to use the restroom. Looking at myself in a restaurant bathroom mirror, I reflected on the Death Meditation and realized that if I continued down this path, there would be many life experiences I would never have. It was the last time I drank, took drugs, or smoked.

Making it through that first year sober, where all the anger, sadness, resentment, self-hatred, fear, and anxiety that the substances were barely keeping a lid on, was a rollercoaster ride. I cried a lot and screamed even more.

Then things began to shift. As I allowed myself to feel and express what had been repressed for so long, I began to balance my nervous system. I began to calm down. I stopped feeling so angry. I started to feel better. I began to trust in myself and others.

As I write this, I'm approaching my five-year sober anniversary. I can listen to my emotions now. Every so often, I feel myself relapsing into numbing behaviors, like workaholism, internet black holes, or emotional eating. When I feel myself getting disconnected from my core self, it's a sign I need to do less and listen more. Put less pressure on myself. Forgive myself. And accept that where I am is perfect. I can live one day at a time.

Weekly Exercise

- For the next week, do some form of movement each day for a minimum of 30 minutes. On at least 5 of these days, work up a sweat (HIIT, a strong yoga practice, running, dancing).
- The other two days, make the movement as still and quiet as possible (gentle yoga or stretching, meditation).
- Ask yourself "what am I feeling?" The answer could be "sweaty" or "bored" or "out of breath." Just feel.

- Then ask yourself "what do I need to know?" and let the answers come from your intuition. Journal your observations.
- At the end of the week, review your journal. Does a theme stand out? Do you tend to experience a certain type of feeling a lot (for instance, "tired" or "annoyed") or do you have a wide range of feelings? What information can you intuitively derive from this process that can lead you to deeper realizations about what you're able to feel and what you're avoiding.

PATTERNS, HEALING, & LIFE AT ITS BEST

Being open and honest about your pain, negative thoughts, and patterns is the greatest gift you can give to yourself and the world around you.

By: Joe Schlabach

Story:

I was jolted awake, the icy cold air stinging my skin. It took half a second for me to realize I was flying through the air, my back burned as I flopped to the ground, and skidded across the frosty floor, my body slamming into the metal frame of my brother's bed. "HOW MANY TIMES DO I HAVE TO TELL YOU, NOT TO MAKE ME WAKE YOU TWICE!?" My father's words slashed through the frosty air waking everyone else in the house. Everyone knew I was being stupid again. Without another word, my dad turned and left the room. I glanced at the clock; it was 4:40 A.M. and my brother's bed was empty. I must have dozed off again! I scrambled to get dressed, running towards the barn while still buttoning my coat.

Life on an Amish farm was not easy. My earliest memories of my father are of him logging during the day and farming at night. The burden of debt and a family of ten children drove him to push his body far beyond what a normal human would. This responsibility was also compounded by the lack of technology; no electricity, no phones, and no motor vehicles. As a result, all of us were expected to do our share and help where we could. This provided the perfect setting for my pattern of self-loathing, shame, and anger to develop itself.

Incidents like the jolting wake-up call from my father, were normal in my life, happening almost daily. I would do something wrong, have someone make a big deal out of it, and I would obsess for hours, sometimes days over how stupid I was, how I could do nothing right. For 30 years every time I made a mistake, I would devolve into a pattern of calling myself names and kicking myself for the slightest mistakes. Thus my pattern of self-loathing, shame, and anger was established and was reinforced over and over again. This self-loathing shaped every aspect of my life and followed me everywhere I went, growing and expanding like a snowball rolling down a frosted mountain.

I finally reached my breaking point. In desperation, I reached out to a friend, who helped me see the worth I carried within myself. My friend connected me to a community that was filled with people just like me, people who are breaking their own patterns, who are facing their own fears, who are showing up imperfectly every day, and loving themselves exactly where they are at. I have watched my leaders be incredibly vulnerable, I have watched them break, I have watched them own their mistakes, and still love who they are.

I remember when I finally realized that I deserved to take care of myself; that living in pain was not serving anyone, and it did not make me noble to suffer unnecessarily. Let me say that again. *You are not noble for suffering unnecessarily.* It does not make someone a hero because they bear their anger, pain, and frustration in silence. Being open and honest about your pain, negative thoughts, and patterns, is the greatest gift you can give to yourself and the world around you.

Society expects men to be the strong silent types. However, that was never who I was; although, I tried, and failed, over and over again. Once I started trying, and succeeding, to be who I truly was inside, my life completely changed. It felt terrifying to no longer hide who I was. I felt like such a loser and a failure; if I showed everyone who I was, my friends would abandon me and I would be even more of a loser. What happened was the exact opposite, yes there were those who did not understand who I had become, they soon fell away, I was left with my true friends, and many new friends who understood me in a way I never knew was possible.

It was not an overnight transformation, it was a slow process, and with consistency and encouragement, I slowly started to love the person looking back at me in the mirror. I still face challenges every day and I still make mistakes on the regular. The difference is what I focus on. Instead of focusing on the things that go wrong, I focus on the things that go right, or as I call them, my wins.

The amount of love and light in the world never ceases to amaze me. For the longest time, I walked right past all the great things happening around me and I never noticed all the little things that made this world an amazing place. Now I make it a practice to notice the little wins every day. I love to take a moment to breathe in the crisp, cold, winter air, the taste of coffee as I take a sip, a smile from a stranger on the street, the joy of a song on the radio, or just the simple fact that I am alive and every day is an adventure.

I did not start noticing these things automatically; it took practice to recognize the joy that surrounded me. Just recently I started a practice in allowing myself to see the light around me even more. At the end of every day, I take a moment to write down every little piece of joy and light have seen throughout the day. Every day I try to make the list longer than the day before, leading me to be very aware of all of the fun, light, happy things around me and to keep looking for more. By claiming the love and joy I see in my life, I attract more love and it builds on itself. In the same manner, my pattern of self-loathing, shame, and anger grew like a snowball, so does my self-love and joy, when I keep consistently looking for the love and joy in my life.

Weekly Exercise

I challenge you to try the same, whether you choose to jot moments down throughout the day or list them all at night, try to make the list longer every day.

- At the end of each week read the lists and allow yourself to feel the feelings you felt when you noticed the moments.
- Breathe deep, connect completely, and feel gratitude for the amazing life you lead.

Work, Life, Meaning, Purpose, Love

While I said yes to others - I said no to myself.

By: Clara Norell

Story:

As I walked up the creaky wooden stairs, my feet scraped heavy against the steps. I could feel my heart pump fast and irregular. I felt heavy. So heavy. Tired in my body, as if I was a hundred years old. The tiredness inside of me was like a heavy storm of dark emotions. I could hardly breathe, much less talk.I saw stars in front of my eyes, was extremely dizzy, and felt nausea.

Still, there I was. On stage. In front of people. Smiling and acting "normal" to the audience, and the the group of people I was leading for work. As I stood there in the limelight, almost fainting, I remember my body trembling, and the stressed out energy inside me when I introduced the breakfast seminar that morning. I could say the words - the pitch about our work organization and our speakers. Working like a robot. My body, mind, and soul were not in a healthy state. Still, I stayed and kept talking, not even hearing what anyone said, and pretended everything was okay. Secretly I was really not okay. As a leader, I should have dared to pull the handbrake and left there and then.

These alarming signs of my mental breakdown came in October 2017, shortly after I was discouraged and hindered from working on my vision of building sustainable low-income hempcrete houses for the marginalized people of South Africa. As I got held back from taking steps towards achieving my dream - I started to feel like I was living a life without meaning. I lost purpose of waking up in the morning.

Along with losing purpose, I also found myself lacking mandate and taking unnecessary responsibility over the shortcomings of others. Instead of asserting boundaries around expectations of my work, I was playing the "good girl". I felt as if I had to give of myself and my efforts, to the point of being totally drained. While I said yes to others—I said no to myself. I always thought I had to be the perfect girl. There was no room for me to fail.

The tipping point came at the end of November 2017,. which caused the cup to drain.

I could neither think clear thoughts nor remember simple things in my everyday life. I felt as if I was not enough. I felt unseen. Unheard. The following week I could not get out of bed. My arms and legs burned as if they were on fire, yet I still felt cold as ice. I could not move. It was frightening. Shortly thereafter I was sent to the corporate healthcare office, where I was diagnosed with acute fatigue syndrome due to work-related stress, and assigned immediate sick leave. I had hit the famous wall. When I look back and think about myself at that time, I can see clearly that I was addicted to this stress, to the pleasing of other people, so much that I nearly worked myself into my grave.

But why? It was a normality for me — putting the needs of others before my own. Being "safe" in a truly self-destructive space. My needs were not important. I actually do not think I even knew what my needs and limits were at that time.

During my six months of sick leave, I suffered from severe panic-attacks, guilt, shame, and fatigue. I was burned out, numb, and groping in the dark. I completely isolated myself, not even daring to go outside. I went from being a vibrant social butterfly, to developing a crippling social phobia.

I remember the day in May 2018 when I officially came back to my office. I was terrified and revulsed by the thought alone. The mere smell of the building made me vomit in my mouth all on its own. It was such a trigger for me. I felt the uncomfortable rushes and waves of panic rushing through my body. My whole body screamed at me to leave. I realized a change was inevitable! I was in emotional pain from the transformational process. Once upon a time, I had loved my job so much. It was my anchor and my identity for seven years.

During a long vacation in the sweltering, sunshiny, Swedish summer, I slowly started to feel alive. Softer inside. Juicy and warm. My mental state was coming in balance with my physical state at last. It dawned on me that I had developed a codependent relationship with my job, and started to explore the signs of being a workaholic.

I knew it was me who needed to change. If not, I would keep sabotaging myself with self-hatred and destructive behavior, which would sabotage any work situation. I finally felt "Enough is enough". I am enough. It was time for me to put me first, at long last!

August 28th 2018 I resigned from my position. September 1st 2018 I signed up for the Little Volcano 3-Day Challenge. Since then, my life has changed profoundly. Today, I dare to stand up and say: "Hi, my name is Clara, and I am a recovering codependent and workaholic."

Weekly Exercise

My favorite exercise for self-love is something I have practiced on a regular basis since I almost lost my life in a surf-accident in Maui, Hawaii, back in 2000. The fin of my surfboard nearly cut off my left leg. Since then, I like to give a lot of love to my legs, thighs and knees. This exercise is inspired by the ancient Hawaiian practice of forgiveness known as the Ho'oponopono—"I'm sorry, please forgive me, thank you, I love you".

For this week, I encourage you to slow down and take yourself on a date. Invite yourself to a self-love spa night at home. Let your body receive some tender love and care.

Soak yourself in a hot bath with essential oils and bubbles
If you don't have a bathtub, lay in your bed with freshly changed sheets
Light candles, burn incense
Put on soothing sounds
Massage and rub your body
Stroke and feel yourself
Tell your different parts of your body—you love them so much and feel so much joy and gratitude for everything they help you through in life
Your legs for walking, running, biking, surfing, dancing, jumping through life with you
Apologize for the times your mind have not been there for them and ask for forgiveness
Then tell them again you love them
Continue to massage and rub your whole body while you repeat the procedure of giving yourself love
Be creative! Allow yourself to receive.Feel the magic sensations of self-love.

My healing is far from finished. Recovery is something that you have to work on every single day and it's something that doesn't get a day off. I have a deep desire within to live more true to myself and dig deep to find out who I really am. What brings me joy.

The hardest for me to let go of is:

- Shame
- Guilt

I no longer feel an urge to:

- Prove myself to be worthy
- Perform to receive Love and respect
- Say Yes when it really is a No

Wins from my self-love revolution:

- When I wake up - I think out loud three things I am grateful for
- When I have feelings of doubt - I respond with thoughts of gratitude
- I work with what brings me joy
- I let go of taking responsibility for others
- I let go of feelings of a duty to open messages before I am ready to respond

The Platinum Rule

Love doesn't have to be any certain way, in order for it to be authentic.

By: Al Fearer

Story:

"How does one describe the ineffable?

I can feel *it coming off her*
A humming aura of pure electricity
A magnetism
When we get close
That silky suave look in her eyes
All we become in that moment
Is the explosive energy of when
Dopamine meets serotonin
Worlds collide
Words cannot describe
Her ineffable touch."

The poem you just read is one that I wrote for my girlfriend (who I will refer to anonymously as "T") approximately one month into our relationship. As you can tell, I am most certainly a romantic die-hard. It's true. I am proud to be a man of passion. I love being in love, and every day, I revel in adoration and admiration for my girlfriend, who is in fact, an *aromantic*—someone who does not experience romantic feelings for others. The staunch irony in this is that the relationship I have with T is actually the first relationship I've had in my twenty-four years of life thus far on Earth—and I am absolutely gaga, bonkers, moonstruck in love with her.

Much like the two sides of every coin, however, there is a polarizing flipside to my gushy romantic proclivities. A very dark one, in fact. The truth in the matter is that I have spent a great deal of these twenty-four years plagued by apathy, nihilism, self-destruction, and self-loathing. I have felt doomed to the fate of some bright yet feckless marshmallow, trapped in the harrows of a massive existential vacuum—forever expanding from internal pressure, only to pop and pitifully shrivel.

The reasons behind this ennui have taken a lifetime to understand, and truthfully, my understanding of it in a perpetual state of flux. I was born an only child to two doting parents who have always been loving to one another other. To this day, they remain the most down-to-earth, giving, and honest people I've ever known. I never witnessed them fight, and I can count on less than one hand the number of times I was ever traditionally punished because I was pretty much a good kid. I say *traditionally* punished because, exactly like all of us, my parents are humans, with human flaws.

My dad was especially human in this regard. The earliest memories I have around fear, shame, and hurt stem from his short-tempered verbal abuse, passive-aggression, and a few select idle threats. With an angrily-stated phrase as simple as, "We'll finish this conversation in the morning", I grew up afraid of my own father. His signature way of holding his fury out on me was how I was punished in the short-term. How I learned to wallow in shameful dread and *punish myself* as a result, was how I was punished in the long-term—and thus began my journey with a myriad of different pains. These pains have manifested themselves in the following ways, in semi-chronological order: overconsumption of unhealthy foods, weight gain, being picked on for that weight gain, unbearable body shame, feelings of social ineptitude, heavy burdens of talent, never quite fitting in, feelings of utterly low self-worth and confidence, feeling hideous and unlovable, belief that I would *actually* die a sad, fat virgin, uncontrollable feelings of inadequacy, swimming in a cold, boundless sea of depression, vicious self-mutilation, casual drug use and eventual crippling heroin addiction, countless rehabs, and finally, many suicide attempts and psych unit stays.

I listed these pains semi-chronologically because one precipitated the next. I also listed every last one of them *not* to demonstrate that I'm some sort of fucked up basket case, but rather to pinpoint one common denominator between each one: *I have been absolutely ruthless and tyrannical with myself.* I have called myself every last derogatory, ugly, oppressive name in the book, and because old habits tend to die hard, living in self-love is something I still must perpetually maintain.

To explain this further, allow me to return to the subject of my current relationship. T has shown up in my life not only as a girlfriend, but (not necessarily by her own admission), an actual healer as well. I can tell you unabashedly, Dear Reader, that I have shed far more tears in front of T than any other being I have ever known. She has helped me break down negative core beliefs about what it means to truly be a man, and inspired me to build positive ones. She has seen me incredibly spiritually sick, taking two steps forward then one step backward, while still supporting me anyway. Most importantly, however, T has taught me volumes about myself and about what it means to *love*, even though we both experience it in vastly different ways. She has shown me unequivocally that *love* doesn't have to be any certain way, in order for it to be authentic.

T and I are both patently gentle spirits, and it is this very gentle-spiritedness that provides a foundation for the wondrous thing we have together. For me, however, a paradox comes into play when I look at the gaping discrepancy between how I treat T, and how I treat myself. *Absolutely never* would I shame her, call her awful names, encourage her to try drugs or suicide, cut her or burn her, because, as I mentioned, I am absolutely gaga, bonkers, moonstruck in love with her, and hold her in the highest possible esteem.

From a tender age we are taught about what is formally known as *Kant's Imperative,* and commonly known as The Golden Rule: "Treat others how you would have them treat you". A noble maxim indeed, and one so simple by which to abide! But, my love for T taught me me a facet of that maxim that even a great philosopher such as Kant could not—*"Treat yourself the way you treat those you love."*

Weekly Exercise

1. Think of someone you are madly in love with. They could be a significant other, a child, a sibling, parent, or pet.
2. Every morning upon awakening for seven consecutive days, meditate for at least a few minutes on your love for them.
3. Revel in this love as much as possible throughout your day, remembering to treat yourself with the same unconditional gentle-spiritedness that you would treat the one you love.

Checkpoint #2

It's happening. Your self-love is expanding and erupting in more ways than one. You are now two-thirds through your journey. Use this fancy little checkpoint to slow down and enjoy your progress.

This is your moment to look back and celebrate how far you've come and to soak in all the rewards you've earned.

It's easy to forget to fill up your tank, to get distracted, or stop putting yourself first, especially as you are nearing the end of a journey.

The antidote to your empty tank is community. This time we challenge you to go further than the internet, and bring it closer to home. Invite friends who are local to you to finish the final months with you or find someone within your community who is already on this journey. Start a weekly book club where you get to form highly valuable in-person connections.

You can find all the resources you need to start a book club from our websites:

Thelittlevolcano.com
or
Therevolutionofselflove.com

Now turn to Checkpoint #2 on page ___ and fill out the questions document your journey.

UNLOCKING THE DOOR TO SELF-LOVE

The key to unlocking the door to self-love is being real with yourself!

By: Lynda Worthington

Story:

Self-Love is something I think everyone is born with, but maybe in my case, I forgot it somewhere along the way to my adulthood. When I was a child, I loved discovering all the wonderful new things I could do. I was so excited to show my parents and siblings how awesome I was! "Look at me! Look what I can do!"

However, growing up in a dysfunctional home made it easy to forget who I really was deep down. I craved my family's attention and approval to validate my worth, instead of ignoring the voices in my head telling me that I would never be enough, that I would never quite measure up, and that I might as well give up!

All throughout my life, I kept looking for people and circumstances to determine my worth and value. I thought my happiness rested in the hands of everyone else in my life! I thought I must not be worthy enough or else everything in my life would be perfect, right? I thought something must be wrong with me because I just felt so miserable inside. I thought I was a fairly good person who tries really hard to do the right things, so why was my life going so horribly wrong?

By the time my first marriage ended in divorce, and my second marriage began to crumble, I had hit rock bottom. I thought I must be unlovable, undesirable, and undeserving of the love and happiness I had always wanted. I began searching for something, anything, to help me understand what I must be doing wrong and how to fix it. I began pouring over several self-help books, attending tons of seminars and webinars, and taking online courses from some of the top life transformation gurus out there. I gained a lot of knowledge, but I had no idea how to apply it, not until I learned the one simple, yet powerful concept that literally changed my life and helped me to finally cultivate self-love.

I already had a personal belief that all humans on this planet actually chose to come here. What was life-changing was learning that we also actually chose to experience all the things that have shown up in our lives, before we ever incarnated here! That meant I actually chose to experience all the good, the bad, the excitement, the trauma, the joy, the heartache, the success, and all the hardship! Every single experience was specifically and uniquely chosen for me, and by me!

At first, I was so angry that I threw the book which first Introduced me to this concept across the room and screamed at it! I was seething at the idea that I would ever choose to be abused as an innocent child! Why would I ever choose to be betrayed by a spouse I trusted? Why would I choose to experience excruciating pain in my body? Why would I choose any of it? The plain and simple truth was that it was all to experience contrast, to comprehend that everything has its opposite. The purpose was to grow, and stretch, and learn that everything works together for my ultimate good. Everything I have ever experienced in my entire life was designed to help me truly love myself and love others.

How could I understand joy if I had never known heart-ache? How could I know health if I had never known sickness? How could I know hot without cold, salty without sweet, light without dark, pleasure without pain? Look to all of nature to testify of the contrasts literally built into this world. It's in the different seasons, in the climates, in the variety of plants and animals, and in the triumphs and tragedies of survival! It's all around us, everywhere! How could I expect to escape from all that life on this planet entails?

I surveyed my life experiences, both positive and negative, and realized that sometimes the stories I was telling myself about them simply weren't true. Sometimes, they were downright mean! I had to learn to be really honest and allow all my raw feelings and emotions to come up and be felt fully.

I learned to accept that my soul is a benevolent being who loves me so deeply and so completely that it would design and orchestrate all my life experiences for my highest good. I understood that I can love and accept myself and forgive myself of my so-called "mis-takes" because my soul knew it would be worth the hard lessons. I learned that I can choose to love others and help them to find their lessons, their self-forgiveness, and their self-love. In time, I also learned to fully forgive those who hurt or offended me or my loved ones because they played a critical part in my growth and in my journey toward more self-love and more love of others.

Of course, my life didn't change overnight, but my perspective did. I still had to do the work, but it was worth it to find the kind of inner peace and centeredness I feel now. I believe it is a never-ending process and will probably continue beyond this current existence. But for now, with each experience I have, I remember that I chose it! Then I let go of resisting it, start being real with myself, and accept that I desired this experience to help me grow in some capacity I have not yet mastered. It is either showing me something new to transcend, or it is reminding me that more work is still needed in a particular area before I can move on, or it is encouraging me to pass on what I've learned to others and help them to move along on their journey.

Unlocking the door to self-love begins by being real with yourself. If you have the courage to turn the key, you will step into a magical world filled with more joy and happiness, more compassion and forgiveness, and greater love and acceptance of yourself than you've ever known. Your challenge is to fearlessly walk through the door!

Weekly Exercise

One powerful exercise I used to unlock the door to self-love is what I call "Being Real in the Mirror" which is very helpful and healing. You're going to be real with yourself and have an honest conversation. No bullcrap allowed!

- Think of 2 or 3 negative phrases you've said about yourself (such as "I'm ugly" or "I'm not good enough," etc.) and write them down in a journal.
- Next, stand or sit in front of a mirror and imagine the person you see in the mirror is the 4-year-old little you. Now speak those negative things to your little self. How do you feel?
- Imagine the hurt or anger you'd feel if someone else right now told that 4-year-old those same things while you were standing there watching. What would you do? Sit with these feelings and write them down in your journal.
- Next, while looking into your eyes in the mirror say, "I'm so sorry I've said this to you! It has hurt you and created negative feelings about yourself. I'm done doing this to you. Please forgive me!" Really mean it when you ask forgiveness from yourself.
- Now flip each negative phrase to a positive one and say, "I am now replacing this negative thing I've said to you." Then think of an "I am" type positive affirmation that is directly opposite of what you had negatively said. For example, if you had previously told yourself that you were ugly, say instead, "I am beautiful just the way I am right now!" Look deeply into your eyes and say that phrase slowly and meaningfully at least three times.

- Make sure to choose a phrase that is meaningful to you, that makes you feel really good about yourself and something you really want to start believing about yourself. Write it in your journal. Then go back and repeat the same process with the next negative phrase you wrote down.

Each day throughout this week, look into your eyes in the mirror and repeat only the positive "I am" statements you wrote down. Record your thoughts in your journal.

I believe that if you really put your heart into this exercise and do the work of being real in the mirror, you'll begin to feel better about yourself and cultivate more self-love and respect

"AWAKENING MIRACLES."

Celebrate the little magic and BIG miracles will awaken.

By: Katie Joy

Story:

I once thought that taking care of others and being a "good girl" was my ticket to being enough. I realized that by taking care of others' needs at the expense of my own, I was trading my attention and energy for someone else's approval and validation of me so that I felt that I was worthy.

What I found was, in the process of taking care of other people's needs, I was neglecting my own. I had been seeking my "worthiness" and "love" from others. And the truth was, in spite of my many achievements and successes by most standards, secretly I didn't believe I was worthy.

In fact, in relationships, I often accepted attention as 'love', which frequently landed me in hot water, choosing personal relationships with men that would first charm me, then harm me. I had settled for a pattern of believing that I deserved to be abused and that I wasn't worthy of love. And I got just that.

UNTIL...

I drew a line in the sand, after one final violent outburst during an argument that escalated with my partner throwing garden tools at me and punching a metal cabinet only inches from my head as a threat to "watch out."

I was so full of angst with fear of not being loved, that I begged for it until that point. That was the point when I realized, something had to change. That I couldn't change him, or convince him to love me the way I needed to be loved. I woke up at that moment to the truth. That I needed to change me, not him.

That journey was dark and deep, as I swirled inward facing myself alone.

I came face to face with parts of me I had forgotten and had disconnected from, trying to ignore since I was a kid. I'd been living with false masks on all my life to be accepted as "good enough", that when I found my true self again, I cried.

As my heart cracked wide open, and I delved into all the feelings, it was scary—terrifying, in fact. I felt so vulnerable. But in that vortex of vulnerability, I rediscovered my power of authentically feeling; seeing, hearing and understanding myself, and loving me.

I shifted from trying to meet my needs by helping others meet theirs. And began new daily rituals of meeting my own emotional needs directly. This was difficult at first. Clunky. Uncomfortable. I, like so many of us, had been programmed and conditioned to believe it was "selfish" to put myself first.

But I was at my rock bottom emotionally, and serving others while sacrificing myself had led to complete burn out. So I decided to pour all the love I had poured into others, into me.

With one small self-love act at a time, my journey of self-love began. What I noticed, is the more I loved on myself —the more I acknowledged myself with what I appreciated about myself —the kinder I became. To me and others. And the better I began to feel.

With each step— sometimes forward, and occasionally I'd fall or step backward in my progress, I would stay conscious of how I was thinking and made a firm vow that no matter what, I was going to love on myself so much until I could pour my love into creating my new life. A new life filled with pure joy.

With each act of self-love, with each shift in my internal dialogue to being kinder to myself, and with each conversation I had, I chose to use loving language. I noticed my energy increased. And with that, my pathway became clearer. At first, it was like a dense fog had finally lifted from my brain. Then, the once choked mental bandwidth (and overwhelming feelings that came with it) was like switching from dial-up internet to unlimited broadband high-speed access.

Like any grand adventure, this didn't happen overnight. But with my persistent dedication to my new journey of self-love, it proved a worthy journey.

As I took action to help myself, I began to teach other women how to go on this journey for themselves also. And like I did for myself, I showed them how to design a new life truly in alignment with her core values, and goals.I didn't wait until I had it all figured out, or felt super confident in my 'whole' life again. I began where I was. And I decided that was enough.

Instead of waiting to celebrate myself for the 'big success' of feeling great and loved, I focused on taking action with my self-love steps to success and began paying attention to the little daily miracles that showed up.

With each little miracle, I began to focus on how great my life is, and that I was creating it, with love for myself first. I literally focused on self-love and gratitude for everything and birthed new joy into my life. And with it, created new levels of success. But this time, instead of measuring success in accordance to other people's standards, I was choosing my own metrics. I stopped evaluating my 'enoughness' based on what others thought of me. And used my internal compass of 'fulfillment' for my soul, each night as I went to sleep. I asked of myself, "Did I give my all to this day, and show up the best I could for myself, even if I was low in energy and tired?" Yes! Then let's celebrate that!

I focused on three to five self-care acts each day. Did I complete them? Yes. I got out of bed and showered. I made myself a nice salad for lunch. I went for a short walk in the sunshine. I phoned a friend and shared how much I appreciate them. I smiled at a stranger. Tick! Success!

I started small. And with each step, I shifted from an almost crawl at the beginning to running and dancing with glee. Because I chose to love me, more than anyone else ever could.

I didn't just fill up my own heart with love. I created an overflowing dam of internal nourishment, that life began to flourish in immeasurable ways I couldn't have imagined when I was coming from a place of scarcity of "not enoughness."

Now I am SO FULL, I flourish and create magic in other people's lives too. Notice and appreciate the little magic and the BIG miracles will eventually appear.

Weekly Exercise

Keep a little daily diary log of all the little miracles that occur in each and every day, and be grateful for them: Notice the smile reciprocated when you brighten someone's day, appreciate the bonus refund or check in the mail, receive the joy of listening to a child laughing. Celebrate the small steps, and you will find yourself running and dancing a mile before you know it.

Recognizing and Cultivating The Internal Mechanisms of a Blessed Life

If you think only wankers engage in self-love then maybe letting go of your hang-ups around masturbation is a good start.

By: Cath Campbell

Story:

Yoga has released me from the angst of many of my hang-ups, making it my deepest expression of self-love. Here, I have found a way to treat my body as a temple and still indulge in—and often enhance—life's yummier offerings. The practice of yoga irons out my physical and psychic creases and cuts my anxiety and depression off at the knees, freeing me up to more meaningfully connect to myself and the people around me. It is my priest, doctor, teacher, Prozac, Xanax, alka-seltzer, aspirin and acid.

In my life before yoga, the nadirs in my path's vicissitudes came from being bullied in school which fueled a sense of anger and alienation. Inherent in the grief at the early death of my mother, was a shocking wake up call at age 16 on the reality of mortality. The internal walls would come down temporarily with a lot of boozy veritaserum, cigarettes, dope, and dabbling in acid and magic mushrooms. Comparing and contrasting this era with my post-yoga life, I don't morally disapprove of drugs, but simply see them as the spiritual equivalent of a get rich quick scheme - that is, if it sounds too good to be true, it probably is! Hence, it is inevitable that these chemicals which are sought out for their numbing effects or instant happiness, will only feed the demons you're trying to escape—including boredom.

In my yoga practice, I recognize that I am worth doing the work. My physical adhesions come unstuck, the anxiety that leaves me feeling nauseous, strangled, and tetanized is released simply via my breath, making me unstoppable—not only in speaking my truth, but in taking the creative risks that entail evolution. The depression that commits me to bed for days at a time is replaced by a lightness of spirit and a groundedness on the earth that simply tells me 'I fucking belong'! I recognize my rights but also feel empowered by my responsibilities. Charles Taylor, a Canadian philosopher, said that lack of recognition is a form of oppression. My yoga makes me feel wholly seen!

Twisting my body into all kinds of pretzel formations changes my perspective on crisis and enhances my experience of joy. The low points in my life are painful nonetheless, but become opportunities to hatch cunning plans, let shit go, and get better at mining for the immeasurable wealth that resides in my internal landscape. This is the vastness inside of me, described by Mark Twain as "the you that is untouchable... what a wee little part of your life are your acts and your words ... [these] are merely the visible thin crust of your world... The mass of you is hidden - and its volcanic fires that toss and boil and never rest, night or day.... are your life, and they are not written and cannot be written."

My yoga aligns the energy of this vast internal world with the external world and knowing that all sentient beings also harbor their own internal world that is just as rich, vast and dynamic, expands my sense of compassion and connectedness beyond measure. Yoga puts the world back on its axis.

Aligning internal & external

Use the principles of science and philosophy to bring more harmony to your internal landscape. For example, two negatives make a positive - let's say two of your traits include laziness and the ability to hold a grudge, direct them at one another so that you become too lazy to hold onto your grudges.

Find resources to sustain you through dark nights of the soul. This could be gardening, playing a musical instrument, meditation/ yoga, running, any creative, physical or spiritual pursuit that helps you process the feeling of lead in your bones, tap your potential and enhances your connection to others.

Compel yourself to flourish by shapeshifting and evolving. Habitually step outside of your comfort zone so that you can handle vulnerability with grace. Be okay with looking like a dickhead. If babies and small children were hung up about how they looked, they wouldn't bother learning to walk because they so often stumble and fall. As we get older, our fear of 'falling over' literally or figuratively dulls our senses and diminishes our capacity to take creative risks. When we remove this dullness we mine our immense potential and find a sense of adventure in everyday life. Most of us view adventure in the framework of exotic, unusual pursuits, like climbing Kilimanjaro, bungee jumping in New Zealand or joining the French Foreign Legion, adventure means you have to wait for a big 'bucket list' opportunity. Yet it can simply be found in a yoga class—try tree pose or forearm balance, or on the street—I dare you to say hi to a stranger.

Love is unconditional but relationships are not. A key to self-love is living in integrity. Keep that integrity in your relationships no matter how much the people you love beg you to lower your standards. This is difficult when you love people who are toxic, bullies, engage in emotional blackmail, or take advantage of your good nature. Indeed some of us put up with rubbish from others because we want to convey the message we love them unconditionally. Just because you lay down boundaries doesn't mean you don't love them, it just means the ball is in their court to step up and respect the love you give.

Guilt and shame are a waste of energy, especially around thoughts and feelings. You are not your thoughts. Our thoughts pass on by - guilt and shame only serve as unhealthy ways to hold onto unhealthy thoughts. Given that you are operating within this vast internal landscape you are free to entertain whatever thoughts and feelings you choose.

Weekly Exercise

This exercise should start to break habits that keep you small, disconnected, looping the same deadening neural grooves. Consider, or better still, meditate on your comfort zone and do something each day to dip your toe just outside that sphere, for example:

- make that doctor/therapist/accountant appointment you've been thinking about but using your doubts as a buffer zone to go no further
- Ask someone out
- Speak publicly
- Have that difficult conversation with your boss/ beloved/parent/friend
- Compliment a stranger
- Hold eye contact a second longer than you feel inclined
- Tell 1 or more people you love and appreciate exactly that
- Go to a yoga class and keep breathing deeply through all the postures you fucking hate
- Sing or dance freely
- Do whatever delightful idiosyncratic parallels of the above—remembering that if it feels weird/awkward/ clunky you're right on track!

Embodying warrior spirit in this way dissipates the prospect of leaving this mortal coil with few or no regrets. Hence the quote "today is a good day to die"* becomes incumbent on making today a good day to live.

Making Love Loud

Self-love is a practice of unlearning who we think we are, and re-learning who we truly are.

By: Amy Dawn

Story:

Loving yourself isn't a job. It's not something that you go and do from nine-to-five, and then at the end of the day, go back to your "normal" life, only to return to 'doing' love the next day, and the next. It isn't a job because you don't get paid for it. I know this would probably change some people's opinions on self-love if they knew a monetary reward would be offered after. Though in that case, loving yourself would become something you do, instead of being something you are - *love.*

What if self-love was love itself? Love isn't what you do, it's what you are. Meaning that whatever you are doing, love is always there; always present, no matter what. However, most of us haven't learned to listen to love, because our pain and our stories are louder. We could easily call this our mental, emotional and even our physical chatter, which is the dialogue that is happening internally and how we interpret this inner dialogue sets the stage for how we feel about ourselves.

My biggest awakening came from years of feeling trapped inside my body. I was so disconnected from it and my internal dialogue was full of hate, disgust, and never measuring up. When I looked in a mirror I felt like I was living a horror story. I rarely remember liking what I saw. I didn't measure up to the standards of beauty that the world had for me. I always wanted to see something better than what I was looking at. Something different, something not *me*. I did not like the body I was living in, and I surely did not love it.

That body had known rape before it was born, molestation by the time it was seven, and on its nineteenth birthday, was raped and lost its virginity. That body always had something wrong with it physically. Then, I identified that body as me, so I lived in being wrong and not enough for more than half of my life. I was always looking for a way to change it or hide it. I had no clue how to love myself, and the very thought of it sounded hard, like a job I wasn't adequately prepared to take on.

At one point my body rapidly changed. I lost of ton of weight, was exercising and eating super healthy. I felt great physically for the first time in my life, for the most part.Then the real awakening began.

My body had changed, and yet I still wasn't happy. I still could feel the fat, ugly, physically inadequate me inside. I still felt unworthy and not enough. I still did not know who I was, and if I was not my body, who the heck was I? Although my physical appearance had changed, my internal dialogue had not.

All of this was leading somewhere, I just didn't know it at the time. Years later after having my son, being physically heavy again, with chronic inflammation, an emergency c-section, a miscarriage at eight months pregnant, having pre-cervical cancer, and a marriage falling apart, my life as I knew it was falling apart too. I was caught in a rabbit hole and all I could see looking back at my life, was one I wasn't proud of and filled with pain. I was exhausted, I was a new mom, and I was living with a body, life and husband that didn't support me.

I felt like I was dying. I totally gave up. I didn't know what to do anymore. I didn't realize my body was pulling me so deeply into itself to lead me on a specific path of understanding its underlying consciousness and energy.. This was the beginning of a brand new life for me. I began learning about belief systems and how they impact the nervous system, and the entire body/mind. I started undoing years of learned limitations, one by one, and it wasn't pretty. In fact, it was the first time I began experiencing listening to the pain inside my body and mind.

To me, self-love is a practice of unlearning who we think we are, and re-learning who we truly are. In order to begin this journey we need to be able to listen to what is happening within ourselves. This means sitting with our body, mind, and all of our emotions; listening intently to whatever we hear, no matter what that is, and choosing to love it. What we typically hear in the beginning is our stories, pain, what we know, what we are holding onto, and our belief systems. When we sit with them, they become very loud and it's often why we tend to avoid sitting with ourselves in this way to begin with. I promise you, it's the shortcut. It's more productive than not doing it. Sure, it might be uncomfortable and painful, but the reward is LOVE. Love does become louder when you choose to listen to the pain. All it wants is a space to be heard, seen and loved so it can soften. Once that happens love becomes louder.

It's like clearing out the noise in a large room full of people, so you can hear the fan. You sit in silence and stillness, then the people become really loud. You listen to them, watch them and eventually they stop talking and you can hear the subtle sounds in the room. Love is like a fan. It may be a soft whisper, but it's always there.

Weekly Exercise

Take the new idea in fully that *it is not your job to love yourself*, but rather that you *get* to love yourself, by allowing love to be louder.

Here are a few simple, yet powerful ways you can start doing this now.

1.) Giving voice to your internal dialogue. Have two chairs. Sit in one and keep the other one empty and across from you. From the seat you are sitting in, allow whatever story that is rising within you (all your thoughts, emotions and physical sensations), come up and speak them out loud to the chair across from you. This is an opportunity for you to dump, to let go and to not hold anything back. Give yourself permission to be vulnerable.

2.) Then switch chairs. The chair you are now sitting in represents love. What would love say to you, if you were sitting in the other chair. Allow love to flow, speak these words like you are the adult who loves a little child. Let the child be you who just finished sharing everything so openly and vulnerably. What would a loving adult say to this child? What does he/she need to hear?

3.) If you don't have chairs, you could also write this exercise out in a journal. So instead of saying the first step. Write it all out.

4.) Then write, what would love do? If love were speaking to a hurting scared little child, what would love say in the form of a letter? Perhaps you could even title this, Dear ___________ (your name), this is my love letter to you.

RITUALIZE TO RADIATE LOVE

Loving ourselves through it all helps make everything make more sense.

By: Emily Polonus

Story:

I was knocked flat on my face when a new relationship I chose to open my whole heart to crashed and burned, when he decided to withdraw and end things abruptly. It was the first time I had fully opened myself up to a relationship in three years since my divorce and I felt my open heart shatter all over again. I felt rejected, betrayed and used. As I caught myself in the midst of deep emotional reactivity, I recognized this twin flame energy teaching me it's time to saddle up to the school of self-awareness, emotional intelligence, and loving my own heart. Afterall, I see his behavior is about his journey, not mine. This encounter entered my reality to fast track me to a higher level of consciousness. As much as it hurt, I see the gift in the divine orchestration at play.

With love, I dusted myself off and asked myself:

What is trying to emerge from me? How can I love myself through this?

I inherently knew: To heal this, I need to feel this.

This was a unique opportunity to show up for myself. And I did.

The weeks following, I dove deep into reflective contemplation and radical self-care mode. Radical, because for the first time in my life, I wasn't trying to push the pain away. Typically in the past patterns of numbing and self-mutilation would repeat in the form, binge drinking, smoking various forms of cigarettes, and dabbling in illicit drug use and the guilt, shame and negative self talk spiral that followed. I've developed a keen knowing that those behaviors do not align with my overarching goal of being a healthy and whole human, feeling physically relaxed and emotionally at ease. I choose to nurture patterns and rituals that empower me.

This time, I sat with the discomfort. I stayed present. I leaned into it and sought understanding and owned my part in it. I could have made a quilt with all of the red flags I overlooked.

The intense waves of emotion knocked me down for a few days. I let the waves wash over me and let the tears cleanse me. I felt my entire being soften with this allowance.

As one of my favorite meditation teachers, Tara Brach always says: "When you know you are the ocean you don't get seasick from the waves." I get it.

I could sense my capacity for compassion and understanding (for myself and other) deepening as I embraced the inner and outer ocean-ness of my being. It's *all* ocean! All connected.

I choose to ground in myself in gratitude and appreciation for the Beauty in my life.

With deeper intention I enriched my days with meaning and purpose by rooting myself in rituals that feel nourishing to me. I moved a lot of my stuff around to beautify and fill my space with sounds and color. I created a sparkle jar in which I record a sparkly moment of each day on a small piece of paper. I spent time cozying up with myself. I poured my heart onto paper, leaned into my favorite daily ritual of intentional essential oil application, communing with nature's divine intelligence. I dove deeper into my study of the powerful emotional benefits of the oils. The simple act of watering and adding beautiful and powerful oils to my diffusers each morning and evening presents the opportunity to check-in: "how am I feeling, and how do I want to feel?" These beautiful gifts of the earth and the immediacy of their aroma anchor me to the present moment and are powerful shifters of mood and emotion.

I reached out to my girlfriends and business partners even though I felt hurt, embarrassed and unlovable. They were there for me, we laughed a lot and through it all, I felt our bonds deepen through true connection. That connection, that is what we all need to thrive. They reminded me how loved I truly am.

My faith and trust in myself have grown stronger than that voice that tries to tell me I am not good enough to be a co-creator, a leader in a self-love revolution or the one that was tries to reinforce the story that I must not be worthy of a loving relationship. I choose to expand past these stories that limit me. They are boring anyway.

My daily rituals root me in the present moment. I feel the embodiment of faith, trust and self-compassion growing through my daily devotion to these nourishing practices, through allowing the intentional expansion of my container and capacity for love and understanding. Yoga, prayer, meditation, journaling, acceptance, forgiveness, leading a team and communing with plant essences all have helped me return home, to myself. I've learned, through these practices and rituals, to warmly embrace all of myself, the shadowy depths and sparkly light, on the path to embodying wholeness.

Along the way, there has been nothing more liberating than standing in the truth that I am not my thoughts and fears but am simply the observer of them. I have the power to choose which thoughts and beliefs to nurture and strengthen, and which ones to release. With this knowing, I more readily release the tendency to grasp onto thoughts (and people and things) that feel less than good in my life. Releasing the grip allows me to consciously choose the good feeling thoughts, look for the lessons experience presents, dismiss the noise and re-identify with what I truly am at my core, to recognize what we *all* are at our core. *Loving awareness.*

May we all remember that faith, trust, doubt, and fear are all like muscles and gardens.

What we consistently strengthen, flex, nurture and feed becomes reinforced.

Through connecting to daily ritual and being there for myself when I need it most, I choose to radiate love... because loving ourselves through it all helps everything make more sense.

Weekly Exercise

Daily Ritual to Radiate Love.

Pair this ritual with a powerful heart nurturing essential oil such as Peppermint—The Oil of a Buoyant Heart or Ylang Ylang—The Oil of The Inner Child.

1. Take 5-10 minutes each morning this week to connect DOWN and IN to your heart.

2. Sit with your spine erect and hands over your heart. (Establishing this connection instantly floods your body with oxytocin, a hormone that elicits a sense of love and inner connection.)

3. Breathe deeply. Feel the space around your heart increasing with each breath.

1. Invite in with each breath a quality of calm and inner ease.

4. With each exhale release any thoughts or patterns that block you from connecting to the truth of who you are. The loving awareness you are at your core.

5. Repeat to yourself: (remember, words matter: we believe what we tell ourselves)

I choose:

To radiate love from the core of my being.
To be here for myself when I need it most.
To trust myself to open enough to ask for help when I need it.
To align myself with supportive people who inspire and lift me up.
To be that person for others.
To love in every moment.

Lather, rinse, repeat as needed throughout your day.

SPICY STARDUST

Why would I be unhappy?
Every parcel of my being is in full bloom.—Rumi

By: Kenna Tuggle

Story:

I have had a habit of being hard on myself, ridiculously, life-alienatingly hard on myself. For as long as I can remember I have motivated myself this way - from a place of lack, scarcity, self-doubt, and fear. I have always pushed myself to *do* well, but in doing so, I missed the opportunity to *be* well. The upside of this pattern is that I got shit done. The downside is that achievements mean nothing if you can't feel them, if you can't actually celebrate them. If you can't actually recognize your own enough-ness and bright Spirit, what is the point? Beautiful experiences - doing well in work/school, climbing mountains, playing in symphonies, traveling - lose their brilliance, turn from big joys to soft suffocations of the soul.

I feel this hardness in my body - it shows up in my solar plexus, the hub of my personal power. It snakes its way around my heart and up to my vocal cords. I feel the tightness in my throat—all the times I swallowed my own power. I feel the hardness in my eyes - my inability to see myself as I see strangers, as a human full of light, potential, love, and mystery. When I look at myself, I lose my ability to see with the eye of love. I see first my flaws, and see second (or maybe third or fourth or fifth, or sometimes fiftieth) my wonder. Why? It makes no sense; I was born to be myself, I was born to love myself.

It does, however, make perfect sense then, that I have also been searching my whole life for the experience of true love and freedom—freedom from this sense of constriction, from the soul-chains I put on myself. You would imagine that freeing yourself from your own chains might be easy - can't you just find some scissors? But these chains can be wily. Though I birthed them, they have developed a life of their own and patterns of their own. Sometimes I don't even know that they are sneaking around my life, energy, and body. The increasingly difficult thing is that if I engage too much with them, if I stay up all night battling them and feel the sweet relief of morning, I can think that I am free, that "victory" is mine. In reality, I poured my precious energy into battling myself. Fighting with my own shadows is akin to fighting a small child, or my dog. In the game of shadows, you lose or you lose.

True victory, true freedom, true home, all lie in a different realm. They lie in the realm of self-love, of stepping into expansive power. I had felt glimpses of this Big Love throughout my life - in moments of deep conversation with a friend, in staring up at the stars, in saying "I love you," on my yoga mat, playing music, writing freely - I knew there was this other level, this other plane. What I didn't know was how to reach it, how to tap into it consistently. It seemed far away, outside of me, as though I randomly and luckily stumbled upon it and into star-world, joy-world, spice-world, fully-alive-world, where energy moves and flows and I could actually *feel* myself and *feel* my full heart; I could actually take a full breath. In this space, my shadows didn't need to be shunned or battled. They could just be. I could just be. It felt like magic. I spent a lot of time seeking this place, seeking this feeling. I longed for it; I wanted to live life inside of it.

It wasn't until I stopped seeking, that I found it. It wasn't until I stopped traveling that I realized I was already home. The key, I realized, was to be present with myself - to be fully awake, to wrap myself in my own honey, my own medicine: compassion and love and full feeling. One of the most profound experiences I had with this practice was through writing a love letter to myself, the love letter I had always wanted to receive—After blundering my way through the first few sentences, I found a groove writing to myself:

You are water, earth, fire, star, every song that has ever been sung, every poem ever written, every sigh ever made, every moan - of pleasure, of anguish - one and the same, you are expression, experience, ecstatic, endless. A day with you is the greatest day of my life, a moment a treasure, a second - I am alight. To have a lifetime? To have many? Nothing is more precious. We have seen so much, you and me, we have been through so much. The wonders and cracks of this planet - the sweet rush of wind. This body, this life is beautiful. I love it almost as much as I love you. But this world is impermanent, this body - ours for a number of years. You? Your soul, your spirit? The adventure of us? It is beyond. It is endless. We have star sailed and will do so time and time and time again. This life is precious. This life is powerful. But don't forget - our work together, our joy, our dreams are infinite.

I love you, sweet one, sweet woman, sweet spirit. Remember to touch the vastness. Remember you are the vastness,

Love,

Kenna

Through writing myself a love letter, I realized I didn't have to *find* anything. I just had to open myself up, to full feeling, to the full power of my own love. I finally discovered what I was blind to for so many years: this current, this magic I was seeking, lived inside of me; this magic *was* me.

Spoiler alert: It lives inside of all of us, it *is* all of us. We are all, in essence, gorgeous stardust traveling through the universe. It can feel a little scary though, to step into your own brilliance, your full bloom. It can be scary to let go of your small I, in favor of your greater one. Our shadows feel familiar. We know them intimately, and staying small means staying safe. However, if we can be bold, if we dare to love, we open up the possibility of stepping into our highest potential, of feeling our full, vibrant, powerful selves. We risk living our full-on spicy stardust lives; we risk finding our true home. My true home, my big joy, my powerful self, is ignited every time I am brave, every time I elide into the current of love.

Weekly Exercise

Step into your own spicy stardust, a two-fold assignment.

1. Sit with yourself and let yourself feel fully. Begin to deepen your breath, and let whatever emotions arise, arise. Notice what happens when you stop running or seeking. Notice what happens when you wrap yourself in your own presence.
2. Write yourself the love letter you have always wanted to receive. Let yourself write freely, let yourself write anything and everything that comes up. Write in a way that gets your whole heart singing. The very act of writing helps activate your brain in a new way, the more processes we involve, the more impactful the message. Take it a step further and read it aloud to yourself, or to a friend, and let yourself *feel* the energy in your letter. Let yourself uptake your own love.

My Child Is Not Mine

As a mother, I feel I know what is the best for my son. But I realized, I was not being the best mother I could for him.

By: Abriani "Niang" Dewi

"I told you not to do this."
"Why don't you listen to me?"
"I told you a couple of times already."
"Why do you keep doing that?"

Those sentences are so familiar for me as a mother, that I continue to say them like an old, broken cassette which repeats with a high tone. Inevitably, those feelings of guilt come right after that high tone falls flat.

"Why do you have to be so angry?"
"He is just a little kid with his own perceptions and emotions."
"He might not understand what am I saying."
"Why must I use this sharp voice?"

What follows is another voice from the inside that beckons,

"I am his mother. What I said is right, and for his own good," and all my defensive thoughts come to make me feel better or to erase the guilt.This cycle kept repeating day after day.

Once I realized that the brightness in my son's eyes had disappeared as the years passed by, I felt terribly sad. He became insecure and reserved, and I could see that he was losing his confidence. Yet, still, the broken old cassette of harsh words still barrel out of my mouth.

There was something inside telling me that this all came down to me. People often told me that meditation was one way to help manage these emotions. When I first learned about meditation, I learned about harmony in everything. But after weeks of practicing meditations, the old cassette in my head still played on.

There was an eagerness to make a change. I didn't want this young boy to become scared of his own mother, I didn't want my emotions to disturb this sweet boy's life, and bring feelings of misery, much like the misery I experienced during my own childhood. I didn't want him to feel the loneliness I felt at his age, and worse, I didn't want him to share my feelings of never being enough.

One day, I awoke and felt lumps on my neck that weren't there before. I was horrified. Horrified that my life would come to an end before I had time to do all the things I aspired to do. Then the more fearful scenario came into my mind—the scenario that would leave my child motherless. Weeks of crying didn't make life easier, and the lumps behind my neck were only getting bigger. I knew that my emotions, my anger, sadness, and fear were eating me up from the inside, and I knew I would have to make a change. But how? I didn't trust a doctor's medicine to heal this condition. I knew I needed something stronger.

I believed in a spiritual higher power that could help me as long as I had the will. I also believed in inner power, so my meditation routine became stronger. I attempted to put worries aside and just accept my situation, even though it was always harder to accept the negative aspects of life over the positive.

I thought to myself, "What the hell, life has to continue, now or never. I don't want to leave with regrets. I have to change. I have to be better." First, I accepted what happened to me. I had these lumps that were getting bigger. So what? It couldn't stop me from doing what I put my mind to. I befriended the lumps, said hello, and that I knew that they were there. Of course, I wasn't overjoyed by this, but, I had to make peace with it for a moment. No more crying over those lumps. No more victimhood.

Second, I began learning who I was. I tried to watch every emotion that came up when something happened, which was difficult for me. I began saying what I had to say and but making sure to not say things when angry. Even when I *was* angry, there was no need to use that sharp tone. I incorporated more stretching, more dancing to loud music, and more ways to get out my head and into my body. Lastly, every time I awoke in the morning, I expressed gratitude for being alive, for having another day, by stretching my muscles to thank every inch of my body.

Once I began to truly understand myself, I felt no worry, only ease. It was no surprise that the aura in my house began to change and shift. I began to realize that I had more control over my emotions than my emotions had over me. That I didn't have to use my old high, sharp tone to express myself.

So now when I come home after a long day feeling tired and drained to see that my house might be a bit of a mess, I make friends with the anger that might bubble up. I say, "Hello, Anger. Let's just sit for a second, maybe have a drink, take some deep breaths, and let it pass." Taking those pauses to sit with my emotions and breathe helped me get clarity and allow me to communicate with not only myself, but also my son, in a kind, calm manner. I can then encourage my son to tidy up the house with me, instead of barking at him as I once found myself doing before.

Months have now passed, and I have found my son has the shine back in his eyes. I remember to hug him tight, and explain that my former anger was not his fault, but my own. I have begun to take responsibility for all of my emotions, and make sure that they don't spill onto my friends or family—and if you can believe it, the lumps have slowly begun to shrink and disappear.

I finally feel like I am enough, and I continue to be a steady observer of my own feelings.
I know who I am and it feels amazing.

Weekly Exercise

Here are a few daily habits I encourage you to try this week to manage your emotions and put you in a more observant space.

1. When you wake up each morning this week, stretch your arms legs, squeeze your facial muscles, arms, legs, your whole body. Let it all go with a long sigh of relief.
2. Make your bed and start to put yourself in a positive space.
3. When your daily to-do list pops into your head, begin by already affirming that every task will be done as long as you have the will to do so
4. Speak the mantra, "May All Beings be Healthy and Happy" out loud, from your heart, to those who you love as well as those that you hate.
5. Always check your breath. When it is not steady, observe what emotions come, then write down your response and how do you feel.
6. If you do become angry, watch your breathing before you speak. Be the observer of the anger.

MIRROR MIRROR

A Reflection to Self-love

By: Claudia Mei

Story:

Twenty-six. That was the number of years I spent in London.

It's what I wanted to do for as long as I can remember. So at the young age of 18, I embarked on my very first solo adventure. Soon I found myself strolling around the streets of London with my square suitcase.

A dream come true and still a feeling of unworthiness was shadowing me.

Everything was going to plan, not without its obstacles of course. I was slowly learning a foreign language, and even began working. I still remember my excitement when I got my very first job as a cashier at McDonald's. Life was good at that time. Two years after, I started a new career in hotel management, and was quickly moving my way up. I bought my flat, had a gorgeous and lovely boyfriend (the first of many), a supportive family, and beautiful friends. Life should have been rocking, right? Yet, I still remember looking one day into the mirror and seeing a pretty young woman, her eyes expressionless. I felt empty and I did not know why.

Something had to change, and it did. I started a new career in finance, ditched the lovely boyfriend, traveled to exotic destinations whenever I could, took up yoga classes, met interesting people from all over the world, and spent one month in India—one of the best experiences of my life. I was leading a lifestyle that many could only dream of.

Until one day I woke up, looked into the mirror and saw that pretty woman again, but something was missing. I still felt unfulfilled and apathetic even though my work and social diary was full, and above all, I felt the loneliness creeping up inside my body despite all the people around me.

The very same day I had a light bulb moment, or so I thought! It was obvious. After years of being alone, I needed a boyfriend, a man in my life to complete me. Thus, my online dating started: Tinder, Fitness Singles, Plenty of Fish, e-Harmony, you name it. I could probably write a book on dating alone, after all my experience with these services.

I spent the next three years looking for my other half, but eventually I could not look at myself in the mirror anymore. The mirror of my soul was sad and lifeless, and I started getting depressed. Even the few long-term relationships I had were a complete disaster.

On the other hand, people around me, especially my parents, were always commenting on how great I did with my life, but that I only needed a man. All this led me to believing there was something wrong with me, and in my late thirties my soul's fire was extinguishing flame by flame. It felt like watching myself turning into an ice statue, utterly emotionless.

A few years later I began practicing yoga more often. This led me to a weekend practice in Edinburgh, Scotland. Little did I know, this trip was about to change my life. I had never visited Scotland, so I decided beforehand to stay a few extra days. On my arrival, after checking in into a hotel, I went for a walk. Passing through beautiful little streets, with lovely houses and gardens, I ended up by the beach. It was a cold and unusually sunny day for that time of the year. After spending a few hours exploring and tasting some of the amazing ice-creams, it was time to head back.

My hotel was about an hour away, but it was a straightforward walk back. All of a sudden, a little voice was whispering inside me, "Be a little more adventurous, go explore more. Go off-road." I thought hearing voices was a bit too crazy, but I followed it anyway.

I felt like a little naughty young girl disobeying her parents, and it felt incredible. I kept going through beautiful green fields, jumping, singing, and twirling, until I got lost around nature, but I still felt safe. A beautiful lake started appearing in front of my eyes and I went closer. I remember feeling surprised when I could see my own body's reflection in it.

My mirror was once again in front of me, but this time my soul was coming alive again. What I could see was a beautiful and sparkling human being. A question surfaced up: What had just happened? For the first time in years, I followed my gut, my instinct and what my heart whispered. This was the very first time I realized that loving myself was the answer. Self-love comes in many shapes and forms, just like we do as human beings. For me, it has been following my heart and not listening to what society expects.

Since that walk, I made the promise to myself that I would do things that delight and compliment my soul with affirmation every day, forgiving the past. No longer would I pointlessly blame myself for things that could not be changed.

It has been a year since my big realization. It has not been the easiest road. Unfortunately, my greatest obstacles came from people I care the most about. When I told them I was leaving my secure job at the age of 45, they thought I had lost my mind! But I have never felt happier with myself and I am now following my dream of becoming a traveling yoga teacher. First stop, Bali!

I have learned that no matter what others think about you, the only opinion that matters is your own. No job, nor person in this world can bring you happiness. It is something that comes from inside you. Like anything else, self-love requires practice, and will improve day by day.

So, tell me -what do you see when you look in the mirror?

Weekly Exercise

Repeat the following affirmations daily, preferably in the morning.

1. "Mirror, mirror, I forgive myself of my past. I am a delightful and powerful human being with lots of great qualities and I truly I love myself. This is what I see every day when I look into the mirror."
2. Write down one thing you will do today that brings you joy.

BUCKET OF FEARS

What the Amazon Taught Me About Life, Love, and Vomit

By: Nicole Piscopio

Story:

First, he handed me a water bottle, then a blanket, and then a bucket. The jungle was so silent around me that I could hear the blood coursing through my veins as my pulse grew faster. It quickly occurred to me that I was scared; I did not want to go through with this.

First, you ask a question, and then you drink. The Shaman went around the circle and passed each of us a cup one by one. I thought it seemed a bit silly to ask questions to a cup of liquid, yet questions filled my brain nonetheless. What was I doing there? Would someone ever love me again? What would I do when I got back to Boston and graduated? I downed the liquid in one long gulp, coughed, then spluttered immediately afterward, my eyes welling with tears as I silently willed the vile liquid to stay down.

People travel to Peru from all over the world to participate in an ayahuasca ceremony in hopes that it will cure everything from alcoholism to depression, drug addiction to chronic illnesses. I wasn't there for any of these reasons; I was there because I was tired of being the cautious girl who was afraid of everything. I was there because I had a crush on the boy I was with and couldn't bring myself to turn back. I was there because I wanted to have an adventure, to lead an extraordinary life. Participating in an ayahuasca ceremony was against everything I believed in; it was scary, risky, illegal by US standards, and against modern medicine. It was a disaster waiting to happen, a potential death sentence in a dark room in the middle of the Amazon jungle in Puerto Maldonado, hours away from my host family in Cusco and my real family in New York.

When the lights flickered off and everything went black, I sat back against the wall and stared at the darkness until the world began to spin. I saw colors, faces, dragons, and fire. I saw newspaper headlines about my death and saw my parents at my funeral. I heard the Shaman call my name and whisper it again and again as I clawed at my hair and my skin in horror, wanting and willing the visions and sounds to stop as vomit spewed out of my mouth and nose and into the bucket beside the zebra-printed blanket. Exhausted, shaking, and covered in sweat and tears, I curled up in the fetal position and scratched at the grooves in the cement wall with my fingertips, wanting so badly for it to end.

I came back to reality four hours later.

"I felt nothing," Jen and Joe both said as we walked back to our cabin in the darkness of the jungle. I struggled to find the words to explain what my ayahuasca experience had been like, unable to fathom why my friends were left unscathed. A few months later I read that the word "ayahuasca" originates from the Quechua language and loosely translates to "vine of the soul" because of its ability to provide clarity and emotional healing. Shamans believe that ayahuasca causes vomiting in people who have something they need to purge physically, mentally, or emotionally. *What did I have to purge?* I wondered during the days, weeks, and months that followed.

The next two days were two of the best days of my life. I felt as though I was looking at the world through someone else's eyes. Colors were brighter, sounds were clearer, my head and heart felt lighter. I felt as though there was nothing I couldn't do, nothing I couldn't accomplish. We spent the next two days playing with monkeys, canoeing through giant water lilies on Lake Sandoval, and drinking Cusqueñas to pass the time during a fierce rainstorm. I let go of past heartbreak, kissed the boy who believed in me, and decided on a career path of public health.

Months passed before I realized that what I needed to purge was my fear. So much of my life had been dictated by my fears. As a child, it was a fear of getting in trouble, of getting caught, of being yelled at. As a teenager, it was a fear of standing out, of being unlovable. As a college student, it was a fear of being ordinary, of having regrets, of being a bystander in my own life.

Moved by the mysticism of the Amazon jungle, I finally learned how to abandon my fears and embrace adventure. While my night with ayahuasca didn't show me exactly where I was headed, it did remind me that I can love myself despite my fears, and I vowed from that day forward to try my hardest to live life unafraid. I might trip, stumble, or fall along the way, but I'll pick myself up, and I'll keep going. Sometimes, we find strength when it feels as though we are lost, when we feel broken, and when we least expect it. What we do with that strength is up to us.

Weekly Exercise

Step 1: Identify and define your fears by writing them down.

Step 2: Understand your fears and how they impact you and your life on a day-to-day basis. Think about how these fears affect your ability to feel content and comfortable with yourself.

Step 3: Contextualize your fears and answer the following questions for each fear.

a. Is this fear acting as a barrier to success?
b. Is this fear hindering your ability to love yourself?
c. Would overcoming this fear significantly improve your quality of life?

Step 4: Devise a plan to conquer your fears.

a. If your fear is something that you do not think you are capable of conquering alone, consider asking for help from your support system.
b. Picture yourself conquering your fears and envision how it will change the way you think about yourself.
c. Don't get discouraged! If you are pessimistic, it is likely that you will not be as successful as you would be if you had an optimistic attitude. If you fail the first time, you can always try again.
d. Take baby steps. You might not be ready to attack your fear head-on, and that is okay. Think about practical steps that you can take to head in the right direction, such as educating yourself about your fear or taking a small step in the right direction.

My journey of finding the purest, highest level of self-love began once I decided to stop accepting orders from fear and started embracing life's adventures. This week, I encourage you to think about your relationship with fear and how it hinders your ability to both love yourself for who you are and become the person you aspire to be. What are you afraid of? Where does your journey begin?

THE DOOR

I step onto the path, not knowing where I am heading, but eager to get there.

By: Patra Healey

STORY:

As I enter the wine cellar, I see a small door. Why hadn't I noticed this before? The wine cellar was one of the selling points when making a decision to purchase the house, but I never noticed the slatted door tucked under the steps. When I reach for the doorknob it creaks open, as if blown by the wind.

On the other side of the door is a dirt path walled by stones. Beautiful plants cascade down the walls with beautiful flowers. Natural light gives the path an inviting and welcoming feel. I step onto the path, not knowing where I am heading, but eager to get there. The light and door fade as I move forward, but I am determined to find the end. The darkness seems to envelop me before I can turn back. Fear and panic take hold thrusting me toward a small light in the distance. Surprisingly, I come upon the sweetest of places. A small room, full of beautiful objects, all having belonged to me at some point in my life. This is both perplexing and comforting. Drawings from childhood, beloved books, and journals line the walls. My favorite doll on display. A small wooden chair invites me to take a seat. Sunlight spills from a window looking out onto the street. The feet of school children, a businessman, a woman with her groceries all rush by. Not one of them notices the wonderful, hidden room just under the street.

All these projects I started with such vigor and joy. A few more stitches here or a stroke of paint there would perfect each one. Until then, they must remain here. I have spent so much time in this room, enjoying the sunlight, watching the passersby. Affectionately, with my gentle touch, I weaved small versions of my heart. Here they are loved, admired and put on a shelf, waiting for their day of completion.

A slight breeze comes into the room and I pull my sweater tighter around me. I stand up to get a closer look at a painted clay pot when I trip over something. I kicked the cap off a drainpipe. As I put the cap back on, I can feel air being sucked into the pipe. The breeze gets stronger as the air moves faster and faster. Drawings flap on the walls, pages of books flutter, the doll falls over and I scream! I grab at things as the suction grows stronger. Fear grips my heart as a whirlwind pulls at everything in the room.

"No, please, don't take them from me. They're mine! They belong to me!"

The whirlwind turns into a funnel, pulling everything from the walls, shelves, and work area, and sucks it down the drain. I fall to my knees as my baby doll disappears down the pipe.

The wind finally stops, walls bare with nothing but dried leaves scattered on the floor. I sob. It's gone. It's all gone.

The passersby continue passing by, taking no notice of the tear-streaked face peering up at them. I pull my body and aching heart off the floor, wipe the tears from my face and wander back down the now dark and dreary path. Finally, back upstairs, I collapse onto the couch with the excitement of getting settled into my new place gone. I am distraught and my heart is broken.

Bang! A commotion outside the front door snaps me back into the present after dozing off. I jump up from the couch and see a crowd gathering on the street just outside the window. An older lady is reaching into a basket on my front step. Where did that come from? What is she taking out of there? I yank open the front door as she holds up a necklace.

"Can I have this?" She inquired.

I reach out to get a closer look. A small gold necklace with a puzzle piece heart attached to it. When the heart is held together it reads "Best Friends". All my childhood best friends have moved on with their lives, but the memories are kept in a special place in my heart, not in the necklace.

"My granddaughter would love this."

"Yes, I think it would be perfect for her," I say with a quivering voice as I move down the steps next to her.

She turns her face up to me, and with the kindest look in her eyes says, "Thank you for sharing. This is exactly what I need."

I lift my head to see everything from that hidden room displayed on the street. People are looking, touching and holding the things I once held most dear. Oh no! It feels like they are reaching into my heart and I am gripped by panic. A woman is holding my doll and tears fill my eyes. I reach for it, but something stops my hand. I hear a voice,

"It's time to let her go. Someone else needs her now." The tears spill over and my chest fills with pain.

"But what about me? I need her."

"There is more for you, but you have to let her go."

I sit down on the stoop and weep. My sweet baby doll, my childhood, all my dreams and fears pour out of me like a heavy rain. The ache in my heart wants to rip a hole through my chest. The tears come harder and the pain lessens as I cry. I take a deep breath, wipe the tears from my face, stand up and approach the woman holding the doll.

Gently taking the doll in my hand, I say,

"This doll is meant for someone special. See her hat? My mom made that hat for her because I rubbed it right off when I was 3. Her poof of hair has been loved to bits and her nose has been kissed away."

Tears fill the woman's eyes. "I had a doll just like this. I used to suck my thumb and rub that little poof of hair. She got lost along the way and I miss her so much."

We wrap the baby doll up in some tissue paper and she sets it inside her purse. The woman grabs me and hugs me with such intensity, whispering thank yous in my ear. She squeezes my hand as she walks away, reassuring me that my baby doll is going to a well deserving home.

Each person approaches me as I sit on the stoop, asking if they can have one of my no-longer-hidden treasures. I mourn each piece, wrap it in tissue paper and hand it over to the life who currently needs it. At times, I feel as if my heart is splayed open for others to see. The pain wells up and the vulnerability feels as if it will eat me alive. But it doesn't. I came face-to-face with vulnerability and together we are discovering a new path. Together we will conquer it all, one small piece at a time.

I was living in such fear of people discovering who I am which kept me locked in a tiny room under the street. By exposing my most treasured objects and sharing them, I learned that I have something special to offer the world. Self-love developed when I stepped past the fear and allowed myself to be seen.

Weekly Exercise

- Take some time, with no noise or distractions, and color the door sketch provided on the book's accompanying website (or draw your own door) in whatever way feels best to you. Pencil, pen, colored pencils, markers or paints.
- Be as creative as you want. Take time to sit with your door and what treasures you have hidden from the world.
- Make notes as you color and feel through whatever comes up for you. Allow yourself to be seen by you.

FEEL YOUR WAY BACK, NOT THINK YOUR WAY BACK

Feel and listen
to what you are already experiencing.

By: Jen Orlando

Story:

Self-love comes from accepting where you are now and appreciating what you can do within your present circumstances. Only you occupy the dimension of your mind and body, and so when you compare yourself to what already exists or define yourself by what you lack or who you aren't, you give that power away. You are not living your own unique experience.

However I put the pieces together in order to share my journey, I realize that the narrative will always sound like a roadmap for arriving someplace, or steps that could potentially be repeated. What I really want to tell you is this: Self-love is a decision that has to be made every day. Just when you think you've figured it out, the circumstances change. The situation will be new, and what worked before might not work again. The path must be rebuilt. The wheel is always being reinvented.

For me, this journey is inseparable from my yoga practice. The mat becomes a mirror for how we do things in the external world, as well as a place to do things differently. We can relax in a way that doesn't reflect how we work. We can step outside of perspectives that no longer serve us, and try new ones on for size. We can strip away our job, relationships, money, and all the external forces that tend to shape our experiences, and instead bare our true selves. My yoga practice is a place where the burden of trying to be something, somewhere, or someone else is lifted. But all this is a choice that has to be made over and over again, not something that is just given. I know this because I am human and I don't always make that choice.

The difference between seeming healthy, versus actual self-love, is a mindset. It begins from a place of acceptance, meaning feeling okay about discomfort, confusion, or other "icky" emotions. For me, this is where the real work begins—not replacing how I actually feel for the sake of self-optimism, and not choosing indifference or feeling nothing over feeling something. This is an act of self-inquiry. Over time this is less scary. Sadness is just sadness. Confusion is just confusion. They don't need to mean anything other than the feeling they carry. You can't intellectualize it, just as you can't tell it to stop. When you accept these feelings, you may notice they suddenly have less power over you. You realize you aren't broken, you are actually responding to your environment. You realize you are alive, and your emotions are telling you as many important truths about yourself and the world around you as your thinking brain is.

Yoga gives us tools to influence our emotional energy through our physical practice. But lately, I put more energy into doing yoga, or anything for that matter, for 30 minutes without expectation rather than "doing x to get y." I start from a place of self-compassion and prioritize feeling good above all else. From this place, I fall in love with the process itself. When I love the process, I can come back to the work with the energy that is required of me to do it on a good day, bad day, and all the days in between. This is where the most valuable progression comes from—the kind that ripples into other areas of my life and to the people I am connected with. This is how I feel alive while simply standing, giving thanks to my body's ability to breath itself and all the other processes taking place with or without my conscious mind. And I care more about maintaining that feeling and less about what I did or didn't accomplish because I know that from this place of feeling nurtured and abundant, I operate as my best self.

I'll finish with something I wish I said to myself a long time ago. Dear Reader, I love you. I love you not despite your messy and contradictory thoughts and confusion, but because of it. I love that you are still here. Not because of me, but because you believe that there must be something more than seeming healthy to others. Give yourself permission to feel where you are in this exact moment. Give yourself permission to not always feel your best at the risk of upsetting those around you. What you give by being your true self is a gift, even if you are misperceived for it. Give yourself permission to mess up. You don't know yet how those lessons will change you and become the groundwork for something far greater than yourself or me. Trust the process, and trust yourself that you are also full of love.

I love you because you value sobering moments like this one, where you connect to the purest experience of occupying your mind and body at this place and time. You want to own your experience and live it to the fullest of your potential. You just have to believe that you already are. You just have to feel and listen to what you are already experiencing. This is the path. You are already on it.

You will lose the path. You will have to rebuild it. I know because I will too. And since self-love is ultimately a feeling, we both will have to feel our way back to our hearts. What I offer you below is not the blueprint to recreate or a drug to simulate. It is simply an invitation to do the work again, and a reminder that you won't be doing it alone.

Weekly Exercise

Yoga and meditation are the oldest self-transformation and self-regulation practices. This process is about going inside and the results may feel like "coming home." Despite this, the practice itself is bigger than any one person. It's like connecting our finite selves to something infinite. For this reason, try to commit to this exercise every day for this week. This exercise is a practice that you will benefit more from with consistency.

1. Find a quiet place to sit. Set a timer for five minutes. Begin counting your inhale and exhale: Inhale for four counts with a slight pause at the top, then exhale for four counts with another pause before you inhale again. Your heart rate might initially rise, but trust in the process and trust in yourself to settle in. After a few rounds of the four-count breathing, let your breath return to a natural quality. Let your body breath itself again.

2. Be where you are by seeing what arises. Don't judge yourself for what comes up. Resist explaining or narrating your experience as a way to proceed unfiltered. Let your experience unfold, moment for moment. Forgive yourself for being distracted, bored, or frustrated. When this happens, bring your attention back to the breath: Say to yourself, "now I am inhaling, now I am exhaling." Use this time to go inside and examine your raw emotions and feelings. You are listening for internal hints of what does and doesn't resonate with you from your present situation and circumstances, but you can't do this authentically unless you let go of any agenda or any answers you think you might already have.

3. By the end of the week or for more regular practitioners, increase the time to twenty or even thirty minutes a session.

THE DOLLHOUSE: BUSTING BEYOND CONFINING WALLS

A Simple Game to Play to Shift Back into Alignment

By: Holly Walsh

Story:

I sat quietly nestled away in the upstairs playroom arranging and rearranging the miniature furniture in the two-story dollhouse built by my father the Christmas I turned seven. I wasn't alone. Rays of warm sun sunlight filled the room warming my back and the back of the gray cat purring next to me. Red ladybugs looked over my shoulder and danced in approval on the glass panes of the window as I experimented with different furniture positions in each tiny room of the dollhouse. Slowly, over time, I added tables, bureaus, teacups, and a chandelier. It was beautiful and magical and perfect in so many ways. Everything was just the way I dreamed it to be.

That was when life was simple and created with the meandering free imagination of a child. Now, Sean was back in my life after ten years of divorce and the cancer diagnosis. This complicated space was strange, confusing and lovely all at the same time. I had learned what unconditional love really was, allowing us to do things together again. We enjoyed each other's company sharing memories and distracting ourselves from the dark place looming just over our shoulders. It felt good the way it feels to be wrapped in an old comfy bathrobe on a cold evening. I wasn't forcing, predicting, or managing any bit of it as I often had grown to do as an adult. I was living in each moment as if it were a gift. I was truly in the flow appreciating each moment. It felt easy—until it didn't.

We had been out walking in the woods bathed in the beauty of fall. The sky was a deep blue which framed the vibrant yellows, oranges and reds dappled on the trees and reflecting in the water. The cold fresh air felt good in my lungs. I was enjoying capturing various shots and trying out different camera settings. We laughed and giggled playing Pooh Sticks on the bridge the way we had when our kids were little.

Sean asked if I minded if he posted a selfie of the two of us. The caption read, "Gorgeous day with my love." My heart jumped. I was startled and unsure what to say. I imagined the flurry of outside comments and questions that would ensue. I didn't want to answer questions or feel as if I was being judged. I didn't want our time to be interrupted by anyone outside of my little bubble. But that is not what came out of my mouth. I brushed it off as if it was as inconsequential as the wind rustling through the leaves, offhandedly saying he could do whatever he wanted and continued strolling down the path in the woods.

My inner compass had been flicked like the spinner on a child's board game. That easy flow was gone. How could that flow be so easy when you are in it, and so elusive when you are not? I moved straight into my head instead of using my feelings as my indicator of alignment. What expectations were being put on a curiously different yet budding relationship? How would my actions or what I said make him feel? What would others think and how would I respond to their unending questions? I felt trapped and confined like a snared animal. Of course, this was a battle reserved only for the confines of my own head. I held the lighthearted outward appearance and at the same time longed for some alone time to meditate and to sort things out.

My chest and throat constricted the next morning as I gazed at the beautiful piece of art in the lobby at work. I had walked past this piece a hundred times. I stood there looking at myself reflected in the plywood and plaster sculpture of a woman breaking through and expanding beyond the walls of a delicate dollhouse. She was too large to be confined by the small dreams that once felt large and complete and perfect. I had grown so much since my marriage ended ten years prior. I reimagined and built a new reality since the old one had crashed around me long ago. I had slowly, over time, found myself, my creativity, my center, my footing. Why now was I being challenged to fit back into the old dollhouse, my old version of reality?

I was fascinated by how quickly I went to right to my head that afternoon after coming to a pretty solid practice of living in each moment. I took a deep breath and calmed my nervous system with a good dose of meditation, it was easy to see my inner lovely wide-eyed little girl kneeling on the carpet in the upstairs playroom. She was scared, reaching toward me opening her hands and revealing the flicker of insight. She didn't speak in words but rather in blocks of knowledge. I soothed her reminding her that we need only to point toward satisfaction to create whatever reality we wanted.

Like most mornings for the past several months, while still in the twilight of slumber, I retrieved a journal tucked neatly in my nightstand and began to write. I listed things that felt good. I practiced this almost daily so the words now flowed with ease. I knew what felt good and what didn't feel good. I knew that my feelings were my indicators of alignment. I knew that pointing in the direction of satisfaction brought more satisfaction.

It felt good knowing that Sean wanted to share how he was feeling. I wrote, "It feels good declaring how you feel" in the column on the right side of the page. It felt good knowing that people cared as opposed to being nosey and intrusive. I wrote, "A lot of people care about your well being and love you." It felt good knowing that things were always working out for me instead of cornering me and trapping me. I wrote,

"Things are always working out for me." I continued writing until three pages were filled.

It felt good to know that pointing toward satisfaction was all that was needed to catch things early on and to shift momentum back toward alignment. It felt good to know that this experience was creating content for the words on this page. It felt good to know that others one day will read these words and be empowered in their own growth with such a simple and hugely powerful exercise. My nervous system exhaled a long, slow breath. I no longer felt anxious, trapped, or stuffed back into the plywood walls of the dollhouse. I felt calm. I felt the warmth of love. I hugged my inner little girl thanking her for being part of my early warning system and reminding me how easy it is to point toward satisfaction. And just like that, I was pointed downstream and flowing again.

Weekly Exercise

Play this simple game with yourself first thing in the morning or when you notice strong feelings.

Step 1 - Sit down and give yourself the gift of time to meditate. Set an intention that you will notice all of the things you are feeling throughout the meditation. This doesn't have to be long. You can do it in as little as 15 minutes.

Step 2 - Draw a line down the center of a piece of paper. Write "Not So Satisfying" at the top of the left column and "More Satisfying" on the top of the right column. Ask yourself what you felt during the meditation. List each feeling in the appropriate column. Satisfaction is like a stick with two ends. When you find a feeling that sits alone in the "Not So Satisfying" column, ask yourself what is on the other end of the stick. What are you learning about? What is it making you aware of? What is it reminding you? Write your answers to those questions in the "More Satisfying" column. Write 50 things or more on the paper.

Step 3 - Fold the paper in half and read through the "More Satisfying" list. Pause to notice how you feel with each item. Carry those feelings with you through your day.

Do this for a week straight and you will notice a difference. Do it for a month and you will feel a definite shift. Do it for ninety days and you will be a different person.

My Heart is Home

Rediscovering My Heart's Joy Through Poetry

By: Emily Olsen

Story:

Inside my head, I hear the words, "You need to get right with yourself, Emily."

I sit at my computer re-reading a poem I wrote in October 2016. A poem in response to a US news report of a leaked audio recording. This disturbing conversation sounded all too familiar to me. Words spoken to me, and many women I have known. You know the recording, the one from the bus.

A Concrete Heart

cold dark room
a lamp
face blurred, name forgotten over time, but
I remember your hands
moving an innocent massage
into tracing of developing breasts

I hate the feel of fingers slow
this was supposed to be a conversation
worldly things, grown-up things
you twenty
me fourteen

you invited me away
last of the lingering party
downstairs, my friend
gone

Is this what it feels like to be

grown up?
hands holding me hard
pulled back
against chest and other things
arch my back
my mouth drops open
catches my tears
pretend it feels good
your grip
getting harder
hurts
my ribs, break one off

I close my eyes

the top of my skull lifts
off
and
down
from the sky
comes water and sand
in helix decent
a brilliant mix of mortar blends
down
into my veins
I trace
it's path
downwards
to my stomach
and girl parts
out
through my arms
into toes
my heart
concrete

My poem is full of resignation. It sounds like I'm giving up. I feel the heaviness of it. A heaviness I no longer want to carry. I'm ready to get right with myself.

I've known for a long time that I need to explore and hopefully heal some painful experiences from my past. I make the call and reach out to a therapist. I don't actually believe I will ever see the other side of this self-loathing. This blame. This, 'I should have known better.' This, 'I saw it coming.' As I explain my story to the therapist, I am annoyed by the length of my list of sexual assaults. Shouldn't there only ever be just one? Two max. For sure only two. I book my first appointment and mention that I don't believe I can ever be healed. He says otherwise. Part of me already wants to prove him wrong.

I begin the painful task of digging up old letters to find my case files. It's been 16 years since the incident that finally did me in. The incident that I didn't write any poems about. The incident that crippled me, the one that robbed me of my self-worth, my ability to love myself, like really love myself. Yeah, those files. After surprisingly little convincing, my case is reopened and I am able to access the remaining 14 therapy sessions.

The next year of my life is indescribable. I undergo the process of Eye Movement Desensitization Reprocessing (EMDR). I commit to weekly sessions with an incredible therapist, a man who proves that men deserve nothing from me, that power and the abuse of power have no place in the room. When my 14 sessions run out, I learn how to ask for more. I learn how to honor what my needs are. It is a year full of pain, a year of which also feels like a return home. I experience peaks of joy beyond comprehension and valleys so deep and full of grief I am forced to acknowledge the voices in my head. The voices that tell me to kill myself. The voices that say death is better than this. I quiet those voices with my new-found strength.

I learn many things during my year of therapy. I learn I can change in a moment. I learn one year out of a lifetime is nothing. Why did I wait so long? I want to scream from mountain tops, tell everyone I meet, 'It's possible to heal, you can, I promise! You just have to love yourself; your past, your scars, your darkness, you're giving up, your losing faith, your 'I don't even know how to love myself.' All of it is possible. And there are ways to do it. There are processes and people who can help. Processes which can guide you along your journey, people who can provide support and love, the same love you will eventually learn to give yourself.

I begin to fall in love with and look forward to my therapy sessions. Having space in my life where I am fully accepted helps me discover other possibilities: my desire to help others, my contribution to my community, being more present for my family, my husband, my children, and myself.

This act of self-love, and the responsibility to take real care of myself expands to areas of my life I never considered affected. My body releases the past, my spirit lets go of all the angry poems, all the self-loathing, all the destructive thoughts and patterns, and in its place, my heart finds its way back home.

A Gentle Heart

a welcoming room
a chair
your guiding eyes
reminding me it's okay

I remember your heart
moving me from my past
into tracing of new memories

I love the feel of letting go
there was forgiveness

gentle things, growing things
you: showing me my inner child
me: listening

you invited me to say:
last of the lingering pain, despair
"they're gone my friend"

Is this what it feels like to be free?
nothing holding me back
I'm me
again, my best self
standing tall
dreaming my heart open
I have no cares
I'm present, it feels good

my journey
getting softer
heals
my ribs, break one off
and I am still whole

I close my eyes...

the heavens open up
and
down
from the sky
come the brightest stars
swirling in celestial decent
a brilliant mix of light and love
fills me up
I follow
it's journey
downward
to my core

my truest being
out, through my arms
everywhere my soul is
my heart
home

Weekly Exercise

1. Read "Wild Geese" by Mary Oliver. Reflect on the theme of home and the idea of being innately good—like unconditional self-love.
2. What sort of creative expression resembles this space called "home" inside you?
3. Spend some time writing these thoughts down (5-10 per day).
4. Let creating a new space of self-love become a daily routine from now on.

HOME

A Journey to True Belonging Within

By: Regan Phillips

Story:

I didn't always like myself. I remember the days I felt so low I couldn't sleep less than twelve hours—more comfortable in the womb of my bed than the bleak life I lived at the time. I was lonely, overweight, poor, and lost.

I'd been asking "why?" Why was my past plagued with deep depression and hidden anger? Why did I feel like I was never enough? I found truth—with a capital T—tongue-tied in my throat, swallowed up by a numbing smile that always replied, "I'm fine."

I wasn't fine. I was drinking more than what I knew was healthy for my body, causing weight gain, high cholesterol, and a compromised immune system that happened with a quickness I couldn't believe. I was sleeping with so many strange men—thank you Tinder for that easy escape. I found myself alone in love triangles, searching for sugar daddies online, waking up next to an emotionless man with rotten teeth and a bong in a dirty trailer. Rotten teeth. A dirty trailer. I remember the day I swallowed my sadness in its pill form and clutched my belly on the bathroom floor while my insides split apart and a life that could have been was flushed down my toilet.

I refuse to feel shame. I lied under the heavy blanket of shame most of my adult life. My head rested on soft pillows stuffed with secrets and regret. It wasn't the abortion that shook me awake. I finally listened to my body when I found it suffering from bronchitis for the fourth time in one year. I swear I could feel arteries clogging in the right side of my chest when I overworked myself, which, at that point, was merely a slow walk up the hill to the mailbox. I was only twenty-four years old and my body was shutting down. I listened this time.

I put my big girl pants on and laced up many shoes on my journey to self-love: vegan shoes, gluten-free shoes, naturopath shoes, running shoes, swimming shoes, yoga shoes, meditation shoes, plant therapy shoes, traveling shoes, and life coaching shoes. It's taken a while to acquire the items that fit, but each one has brought me closer to what I know to be the self-worth and acceptance I've found for myself today.

I wonder how many people on this planet have truly discovered love for themselves. I had no idea what that felt like for almost three decades. I have a list of what self-love means to me. Self-love is doing the most minimal, involved, meaningful thing I'm capable of each day. Self-love is investing in myself. It's giving myself a head massage when I'm lying in a puddle after a sweaty yoga class. It's hearing every love song as a poem written for me by me. It's turning down a relationship that I know deep down is only a sexual one and will never be more than that. Self-love is asking for help when I'm sick. It's knowing I am the one who picks me up. I am my own medicine. I am whole.

I fell in love with myself five weeks ago. I returned home from a recent trip abroad on a spiritual journey of self-discovery. There were a lot of "aha!" moments, epiphanies and revelations about who I thought I was and who I wanted to be. I shed the burdening weight of shame and guilt I'd been carrying. I learned the terrifying amount of courage it takes to stand up for myself. I started pleasing myself before others. I discovered my vision. I connected with my body and soul in ways I still can't even understand. I received a lifetime of lessons in one trip.

It wasn't until my return flight was en route to Los Angeles when I thought about what coming home would mean for me. I've taken so many return flights where I cry my eyes out because of the loss of the place I was leaving and the heavy dread I felt coming home. I never wanted to land on the ground I called "home." I was always looking for that safe place in someone else's culture, someone else's problems or someone else's bed. There was a shift on this flight. I didn't cry and my heart felt the healing it needed.

I knew it in that moment. I was ready to be home because as cheesy as it sounds, I'm always home. In the middle of the night, on an airplane soaring somewhere above the Atlantic Ocean, I celebrated myself as my own home and wholeheartedly believed it. And the world expanded. I was everywhere and nowhere as the skin melted from my body and I felt my own light shining through. I felt rooted and infinite and cosmically connected to all of the worlds within myself. As I connect to that feeling now, I know I can live here forever. I am home. I am magic. I am love. And so are you.

Weekly Exercise

1. Choose someone or something you love so unconditionally that your heart aches, your eyebrows raise and you say "oh my goodness!". You could cry, you want to squish that person or thing because you love them so much that just being around them doesn't satisfy you, like you wanna crush them with your enveloping love and adoration and attention, your body bright with light for this being. Maybe it's your child, your best friend, Jiggly Puff, or the little piglet French bulldog that lives down your street.

2. Describe that person. Why do you love them? What qualities do they have that you admire? How do they make you feel? If they did something wrong, could you forgive them?

3. Now, simply, cross out their name and replace it with your own. Change the pronouns to "I." Reread your writing and embrace it. YOU are the person your heart aches for so much you could cry. You are your own light. Even if you don't believe it at first, it's about the possibility. If you believe in possibility, you believe in love.

Striving for Nirvana

Embrace the sublime tragedy of Self-Love, the most wonderful of hypocrisies.

By: Mike Fawcett

Story:

To write about my journey of self-love feels inconclusive. It seems to imply some degree of finality to it, as if I've accomplished an end goal. As if 've reached a pinnacle of self-love. That my life, my happiness, my fulfillment, is all within my grasp, and despite the adversities I've faced, I've championed through them, and have reached this enlightened state, filled with the love of the self. I promise you, I haven't.

That's the tragedy. If you're anything like me, you're searching for that moment. That feeling that everything is okay. Your arduous journey is complete and the darkness that has enveloped you for so long will never return. I'll be honest, I've obtained inner peace. I've had moments of pure, self-love. An acceptance of who I am, for all my flaws, acknowledging all the wondrous things I have to offer. I've been able to look in the mirror, proud, happy and in love with myself. It's overrated and fickle.

I've suffered through depression during my life. I don't tend to acknowledge it, somehow I feel it'll make me seem weak. Yet when others confide in me as such, I view them as strong, as vulnerable as open. I do not share this same vision of myself.

I can probably count on one hand the times I've openly admitted to a person that I suffer from depression. To the point where I have not even brought it up to a doctor, or any of the like. When the dark thoughts come in, I let them. They consume me, and I feel their heft. That was a larger portion of my formative years. It's been a larger portion of my life. I still struggle with it.

The important lesson of self-love that does not always resonate, is that all these dark thoughts are part of the over-encompassing person that is "you" that deserves to be loved. This darkness, this self-hatred, it too deserves love. That lesson is not something that can be told to you. I've had it taught to me hundreds of times, in just as many different ways, over and over. I had to find the conclusion myself. *You* have to find that conclusion yourself.

I can give you poetic ideas. I can give you evidence. There's actually scientific proof that you are made of stardust. You know, stars? The unfathomably gigantic floating explosions that light up the sky and last for thousands of your lifetimes. You're made from the same material.

Not only that, but you are stronger than them. You're smarter than them. A star has no consciousness. No survival instinct. If a star were to be swallowed by a black hole, it would simply accept it's fate. But you, blessed with life, have the option to defy this fate. To cling to your existence.

You are greater than a star. Greater than something you cannot even fathom. This is the purest truth, and there is no arguing it. Yet, if you're like me, this sacred knowledge will not stop you from feeling the darkness. From feeling worthless. From feeling like you do not deserve this existence. I'm here to tell you, that you don't need to feel self-love all the time. You don't even need to feel it once. But your most vicious thoughts do not change the truth. You are wrong, even when you feel so dark. You are worthy of love because you feel hate for the self.

Makes sense? Of course not. It doesn't have to. It is our greatest blessing as humans to exist as two separate states simultaneously: to hate oneself and to love oneself at the same time. That is a gift. That is our truest state. That is the lesson I have to offer.

By saying, you are perfect, exactly as you are, you are perfect, *exactly* as you are. Even in a state of hatred. *That* is self-love. You don't have to keep going with pure acceptance and love and a shining beautiful tapestry following behind you. You just have to keep going. You could be clawing your way across the path, covered in scars and blood and bile. You can be broken, beaten, and bruised. You just have to keep going.

The pendulum always swings back. You will hate yourself, and you will love yourself. But the true you, that is you, will be unaffected by both.

> You, are okay.
> You are loved.
> You are always loved.

Weekly Exercise

When you find yourself in a place of darkness, simply study it, without intention or desire to fix it. Ask yourself, curious questions, and understand it. Investigate it. scrutinize it. Make it your life's journey to understand yourself. That is the essence of my self-love.

> "Where is this darkness stemming from?"
> "When was the last time I felt this darkness?"
> "What moved me past it, last time?"
> "How does this serve me?"
> "How can this darkness empower me?"
> "How can I be at peace with this if it never goes away?"
> "How can I love myself, if this darkness never goes away?"
> "Where am I still? Where am I in motion?"

Find a sensation that brings you a familiar sense of peace. A taste, a touch, a sound, a smell, a sight. Connect your senses with a moment or moments where you felt love of the self. Where you felt inner peace. If you don't have one, choose to make one. Create a new sensation that gives you that moment of love.

For me, I choose a sound. I chant the Maha Mantra.

> *"Hare Krisna, Hare Krisna,*
> *Krisna Krisna Hare Hare,*
> *Hare Rama, Hare Rama,*
> *Rama Rama Hare Hare."*

The words above, are the names of the divinity that I have adopted. I find that it's not about the worship of any deity. In fact, if anything, it's a worship of the divinity that lies within me. Something greater than the self. That ideal of self-love.

I don't have to say the words right. I don't have to even say the words at all. All I have to do, is acknowledge the wonderful being that is the "me beyond me." The Maha Mantra, for me, serves as this reminder. That I, that you are an integral piece to the journey of this world. You have a part to play in it. And no one can play it other than you. On the days you hate yourself the most, choose to love yourself anyway.

What a Difference a Year Makes

It's two hours before we send the final draft of this book off for formating. I've been admittedly avoiding the ending of this book.

How do I honor all of you, the authors, and this experience?

I'm trying to imagine all the readers who made it to this moment.

A year has passed, and what a year it has been. This journey in self-love has undoubtedly changed so many lives.

So, how do you wrap up a journey that never ends?

The first half of the answer is actually quite simple: start at the beginning and reweave the memories, adventures, hardships and growth you have achieved so that they can form a beautiful tapestry for you to admire.

Today you get to zoom back and see the full picture that you have painted in this short year, so that you can understand just how magnificent you are.

In the beginning of the book, and throughout the book I asked you to flip back here to assess where you were at, and fill in your landmarks and milestones.

And now you get to look back with gratitude, awe, wonder, and a big heaping dose of "I'm fucking awesome."

Today, you get to see your own before and after. Continue reading to see the journey you've been on from start to finish.

REFER HERE TO FINAL SNAPSHOT FILL IN YELLOW PAGE NUMBERS FROM THE CHECK POINTS

THE BEGINNING SNAPSHOT

Date:

Questions:

1. My current biggest struggle with loving myself is:
2. The emotions I constantly feel are:
3. After finishing this journey, I'd feel complete if I could:
4. What do I do now that impacts my love for myself in positive ways:
5. These are the things in my life that I would like to shift as a result of my commitment to self-love:
6. Why is it important that I do this now?

CHECKPOINT #1

Date:

Questions:

1. My current biggest struggle with loving myself is:
2. The emotions that have shifted for me so far are:
3. What am I capable of doing that wasn't possible before?
4. What is one exercise I have completed that has impacted the way I love myself:
5. These are the things in my life that are shifting as a result of my commitment to self-love:
6. Why is it important for me to keep going?

CHECKPOINT #2

Date:

Questions:

1. My current biggest struggle with loving myself is:
2. The emotions that have shifted for me so far are:
3. What am I capable of doing that wasn't possible before?
4. What is one exercise I have completed that has impacted the way I love myself:
5. These are the things in my life that are shifting as a result of my commitment to self-love:
6. Why is it important for me to keep going?

The End: Final Snapshot

Date:

Questions:

1. My current biggest triumph I've had with loving myself is:
2. The new emotions I experience regularly are:
3. Now that this journey is complete, where and how do I want to grow?
4. What will I take forward that will continue to impact my love for myself in positive ways?
5. What are the biggest shifts in my body, mind and spirit as a result of my commitment to self-love?
6. Why is it important for me to keep going?

NEW BEGINNING

So, how do you wrap up a journey that never ends?

Look back and see this incredible web of transformation that you've woven. Take a moment to read everything you wrote and celebrate it all. You will be surprised where you started and where you are now.

Now that you are here standing on the edge of closing this journey, where do you go from this point?

You start new on a new square. Take all the threads that you've anchored into this year, and weave them into the next. You create something new, pulling forward from the strength and lessons of the past.

This is the end. Take a deep breath of gratitude, feeling the completion of this process. Take all that energy you've condensed and processed and dream up the next level of transformation that awaits you.

We hope and pray that your new beginning meets with us somewhere along the road in the near future. Someday we will see you on the street and hear about your adventures, or read them as a chapter in a future book, or witness an ever-expanding breakthrough in person at an event.

We celebrate you and send you off with so much love and gratitude, and one last piece to the puzzle.

Love,
Kit and Rosie Volcano and The Little Volcano Authors Collective

The New Beginning:

You started off with a commitment, and today is simply another re-commitment.

I ______________________ commit to a year long journey of loving myself in new ways that honor the expanded being that I am always becoming.

X____________________________________

If you wish to continue with us as your guides, here are some new ways that you can continue your journey with us:

Celebrate in person. Upon the completion of this book, there will be local book launches for the next year's book. These events are not just for the book launch, they are also celebrations for your completed journey.

Join an event where you can meet others who are finishing their journey and send others off on their way.

Commit to another year in The Revolution of Self-Love with all new stories, authors and exercises.

Write a chapter in the next book.

Come to one of our live transformational coaching events.

Join a coaching program with The Little Volcano.

Work with one of the authors in the book. All of their information is listed on the website.

You can find out about all of these opportunities on our websites:

Thelittlevolcano.com

Therevolutionofselflove.com

ACKNOWLEDGMENTS:

We give our extra special thanks to:

The Entire Volcano Universe (All of our clients, community, coaches, and mentors),

Lola Rephann's Mother

Kailey Mikel Taylor

Craig Holm

Kevin Dungey

Matthew Daniel Royce

Katie Swartz

Yoga Fam

Peyton Theodore Stephens

Ana Forrest

Taylor Howell

Family of Sekolah Cipta Cendikia Bogor Indonesia

Bella

Connor Campbell-Dawe

Izak-Zion & Indigo

From Jambo Truong: The people I've worked with over the years

Esther Hicks

Kyle Cease

CelBel

Dadoo

Pat & Toni Healey

Kirsten Wabbel